COMMUNITY THEATRE

Idea and Achievement

COMMUNITY THEATRE
Idea and Achievement

by **ROBERT E. GARD**
Director, The Wisconsin Idea Theatre

and

GERTRUDE S. BURLEY
Instructor, The Wisconsin Idea Theatre

GREENWOOD PRESS, PUBLISHERS
WESTPORT, CONNECTICUT

Library of Congress Cataloging in Publication Data

Gard, Robert Edward.
  Community theatre.

    Reprint of the ed. published by Duell, Sloan and
  Pearce, New York.
    Bibliography: p.
    1. Theater--Little theater movement. 2. Thea-
  ter--United States--Directories. I. Burley, Ger-
  trude S., joint author. II. Title.
  [PN2267.G28 1975]   792'.0223   73-19113
  ISBN 0-8371-7304-3

Originally published in 1959 by Duell, Sloan and Pearce,
New York

Reprinted with the permission of Robert E. Gard

Reprinted from an original copy in the collections of
the University of Illinois Library

Reprinted in 1975 by Greenwood Press,
a division of Williamhouse-Regency Inc.

Library of Congress Catalog Card Number 73-19113

ISBN 0-8371-7304-3

Printed in the United States of America

For all the workers who envision
a greater American theatre arising
from American communities everywhere.

FOREWORD

This book was prepared as a result of a twenty-thousand-mile journey made specifically to visit American and British Community Theatres. Personal viewpoints were sought on a number of subjects of vital importance to the local theatre both in the areas of management and as a whole movement.

The conversations reproduced here were selected from a far larger number as fairly representative of the opinions of leaders from a variety of places. It seemed pertinent to let the leaders speak for themselves. The conversations were kept as nearly verbatim as possible, and the editors have removed only those portions which were mildly digressive or repetitious. To preserve the authenticity of the statements, undue refinement has been avoided. The conversations were collected by tape recording. In them, particular emphasis was placed on the questions and problems of professionalization of the Community Theatre, community relations, playwriting, subsidy, and leadership.

Two historical conversations are included. Professor Allen Crafton relates the events connected with the founding of the Prairie Playhouse, Galesburg, Illinois. This account tells the story of a pioneering theatre in the golden year of American Community Theatre beginnings—1915.

Eric Salmon's account of Community Theatre in Great Britain broadens the scope of the whole subject and narrates important foreign roots and subjects.

This book is not meant to be a history of the movement, but rather an estimate of its state-of-being in the words of important personalities—all engaged in action.

ACKNOWLEDGMENT

Acknowledgment is gratefully made to the Rockefeller Foundation, Division of Humanities, for aid in collecting material; to the many persons interviewed in American Community Theatre who were not included; to Ruth Hawks, Ora Barry, and Birdene Axling of the Wisconsin Idea Theatre staff.

CONTENTS

I OVERVIEW

Overview   3
Roots of the Idea   6
American Beginnings   9
One Significant Early Group   12
Idealists for the Idea   15
The Awakening in the United States   17
Roots in Education   18
A Note on Courage   21
The Idea of Community Theatre in Retrospect   26

II CONVERSATIONS

Galesburg, Illinois: Allen Crafton   29
Pittsburgh, Pennsylvania: Fred Burleigh and Richard
    Hoover   35
Shreveport, Louisiana: John Wray Young   47
Great Britain: Eric Salmon   58
Chicago: Jack Higgins   66
Erie, Pennsylvania: Newell Tarrant   71
Cleveland, Ohio: Frederic McConnell   82
Omaha, Nebraska: Kendrick Wilson   96
Tulsa, Oklahoma: Theodore Viehman   105
Oklahoma City, Oklahoma: Mack Scism   121

Dallas, Texas: Ramsay Burch   124
Fort Wayne, Indiana: Theodore Sizer   131
San Francisco, California: Jules Irving   136

BIBLIOGRAPHY   145

A REPRESENTATIVE LIST OF AMERICAN COMMUNITY
  THEATRES   150

COMMUNITY THEATRE

Idea and Achievement

I. Overview

COMMUNITY THEATRE is the very front skirmish line in the battle of the theatre arts to overcome public apathy and to gain, or regain, their proper share of the attention of the people. Community Theatre is essentially theatre at the local level, amateur or volunteer in origin and spirit, yet not necessarily nonprofessional; for indeed the contemporary Community Theatre is professionalizing in certain places without necessarily giving up its local roots and volunteer dependence. Community Theatre, broadly interpreted, has a history so old that it is lost in the shadowy beginnings of drama as a part of the human experience, for the communal forms of drama exist in the primitive expressions of all peoples.

The movement is spread throughout the world in a variety of places so diverse that it is impossible to generalize about the size of place or nation in which Community Theatre seems to flourish. It has been known to do well in communities of under one hundred persons, and its success in the great cities of the world is well known. As a national movement it is influential in the United States, Great Britain, France, Finland, Switzerland, Italy, Austria, Canada, Denmark, Germany, Holland, Sweden, Norway, Belgium, Australia, and other nations. There is a fine Community Theatre group in little Monaco and one in the small Duchy of Luxembourg. The entire movement is joined in a generally sincere desire to create artistic works, though the variance in approach and result is extremely wide. The basic problem seems to be the finding of proper means to develop the idea of contemporary Community Theatre

3

as a great cultural and artistic force rather than as a mere recreational adjunct to community living.

At the time of this writing there are a large number of persons
engaged in Community Theatre work. The human material for
successful Community Theatre seems to be endless, and in places
where outstanding leadership has appeared the Community Theatre
has often settled into a pattern of permanent worth. The best examples of permanent growth in artistic terms seem to be those
where there have been one or more notable individuals involved.
Where a group itself has attempted to be the leader, the focus always on a so-called democracy of leadership, the result has almost
invariably turned out to be a weak one, though hundreds of surviving examples of this kind of leadership do exist.

The most serious condemnation of recent American Community
Theatre is that it has not been very creative and has had too little
aspiration to become creative. The Community Theatre seems
infected with the same disease that is ravaging other aspects of the
theatre arts in America at the present time. Community Theatre is
too willing to conform, to pander, to take a condescending attitude
toward new or indigenous plays, to overemphasize the values in
group and recreative activities, to become a mere springboard for
local egos.

Of all these accusations, the most serious are probably those of
conformity and noncreativeness, for certainly the movement cannot
advance so long as it remains a reflection of original work done
elsewhere.

Robert Edmond Jones, commenting on this point, said in a
public lecture: "The art of the theatre in this country is very hard
to find. We've come to be satisfied with a very inferior grade of
goods; we miss the qualities that give a noble turn to things. We
miss the freshness, the caprice, the splendor, the austerity, the
elevation. Yet these extravagant qualities are the lifeblood of the
theatre, the vital fluid. What is called realism is usually a record of
life at low ebb, viewed in the sunless light of day. Perhaps the most
striking symptom of the theatre's failure to keep abreast of the
times is the way we must take efficiency and expertness for true
creation. Audiences have capacity for feeling that no dramatist has
ever touched. We should abandon the theatre whose natural con-

dition is fear and move into a theatre whose natural condition is ecstasy."

Expertness and efficiency there are in plenty in the American Community Theatre. Production is often easily on a level with the best college productions, and many times it is as efficient as the professional theatre. What seems to be lacking is an art consciousness strong enough to transcend fear of failure, which is the fear that really underlies Community Theatre production. It is a fear of financial failure, of community censure, of loss of prestige. There is in the Community Theatre at the present time too little of what is its essential idea: that theatre should become a necessity in American life in terms of art fulfillment and not merely remain a community frill to be turned on and off for purposes of providing recreation or exercises in efficiency and management.

The original ideas of the founders of Community Theatre included the words "joy, creative, native, something in and above ourselves, fearlessness, high standards, freedom from mediocrity." These words and phrases symbolize the shortcomings of the American Community Theatre today, for certainly mediocrity is much more evident than superb work. Yet the urge is there more strongly than ever to develop theatre in the community; and the urge and the result, imperfect as it may seem to be, cannot be ignored. Much of what follows in this book illustrates the valiant efforts of dedicated men and women in America to overcome imperfections in American Community Theatre as it stands now.

ROOTS OF THE IDEA

The recorded history and philosophy of Community Theatre, as the entity which we know today, have been somewhat disguised by inclusion in the history of the "noncommercial" theatre movement as a whole. The art theatre, the educational theatre, the experimental theatre, and the Community Theatre have often been grouped together under the title "little" theatre. While this is no longer so, it is the chief reason why Community Theatre has received small attention as a special development with unique features. The uniqueness of Community Theatre lies in its dependence upon the particular community in which it has its roots, and in which it conducts theatre activity by involving as much of the community as possible. It is related to the college theatre, the experimental theatre, and the professional theatre; but the chief function of Community Theatre is to expose a community to continuing living theatre, and to provide a participation outlet for such theatre talents as may exist in a particular community.

Throughout the great period of Greek classical drama the method and atmosphere of stage production were more nearly allied to those of community drama as we know it than to the modern professional theatre. The same may be said of the drama in medieval times. In both periods stage production was not primarily the work of a definite class of professional stage workers or managers, it was undertaken by a whole community as represented by the city-state in Greece or by the church or the trade guilds in medieval Europe.

The roots of most early American cultural developments came from transplanted cuttings out of Europe. Community Theatre is no exception. It is well known that in the nineteenth century, on

6

the Continent and in Britain, there came into existence a different kind of drama—a kind of upsurging of creativeness, which produced a new kind of theatre art.

The surge of desire for a new theatre seemed to rise in the European countries almost simultaneously in the late nineteenth century. Romain Rolland in France desired a theatre of the people. He said that people are like a woman: they are actuated not by reason alone but rather by instinct and passion, and these must be nourished by the theatre. The function of the people's theatre, far from encouraging sluggishness of mind, is to combat it unceasingly, and present to the people material within the frame of their own reference.

In revolt against stereotypes, conservatism, and purely business considerations, a number of brilliantly motivated leaders brought into being, in unrelated parts of Europe, small theatres dedicated to dramatic experimentation that would appeal to the people at large. The new art-theatre approach to drama which they illustrated was made possible by designers, directors, actors, and technicians who worked together to establish an artistic and imaginative simplicity which at once provided a spiritual bond between the audience and the theatrical creation. Participants on both sides of the stage enjoyed an aesthetic experience that was sustained, from production to production, by experiment with themes related to the society of the day.

The inspiration of the Abbey Players in Dublin permeated the beginnings of amateur theatre in many places. The founders were wise enough to use the works of their own poet-playwrights, whose talents were devoted to writing about the people among whom they lived.

These wise Irish leaders, having had experience abroad, knew that a state theatre must not be a theatre that is applied to the community from without or from above; it cannot be merely the perfected dream of artists; it must spring from the dreams and needs of the everyday person, the need for expression of a whole community.

Of all the European theatres that have influenced our own, none seemed to have fired the American imagination as did the Irish Players. When W. B. Yeats visited the United States in 1903 on a lecture tour, he was cordially received everywhere. In 1911, the

Irish Players themselves came and played the whole country, spreading the ideals of naturalness and simplicity. Their tour aroused the antagonism of American citizens against the feeble productions of the commercial theatre, and seemed to be the catalyst that caused countless dramatic groups to germinate all over America, as a protest against commercial drama. The present success of Community Theatre in America perhaps owes its greatest debt to the Irish Players.

AMERICAN BEGINNINGS

Credit for the term "Community Theatre," as a recognized term applied to a specific subject matter, apparently dates back only to 1917, when Louise Burleigh of Boston wrote a small book entitled *The Community Theatre in Theory and Practice.* She defined the subject as "any organization not primarily educational in its purpose, which regularly produces drama on a noncommercial basis and in which participation is open to the community at large."

Percy MacKaye, a pioneer of the people's theatre in America, wrote in the preface to Miss Burleigh's book: "I referred to the civic theatre as the efficient instrument of the recreative art of a community; our meanings are the same, but I think community theatre is the better name for the same idea. You aptly describe it as a 'house of play in which events offer to every member of a body politic active participation in a common interest.' "

A current definition would need to be broader, for Community Theatre in the best American examples is organized theatre which is localized in a particular community and depends upon that community for its artistic and material existence. The extent of such dependence may include complete public participation in the sense that the process of playmaking is open to any volunteer; or the group may be professional in nature in that all or part of an acting or producing staff is employed. The essential consideration is the necessary involvement of the community itself in the well-being and continuation of the group as a recognized community enterprise in which the citizens take pride, and to which they may look for theatrical entertainment of a better-than-average kind.

If the term itself is of fairly recent wide usage, however, the

9

idea of active participation in a common interest is not a new idea in theatres in American communities.

There have been many early amateur dramatic organizations which have come and gone, leaving little or no record of their activities. Most of these groups were not true Community Theatres because the membership in them was too restricted, sometimes even exclusive. They were really just private clubs, but they were important because they did offer opportunity for participation in theatrical activities to a limited portion of their respective communities.

Not until the period immediately preceding the First World War did the Community Theatre movement show signs of serious growth and development. There were, fortunately, many people who were willing to pioneer for theatre, who felt strongly about experimenting with new methods of direction, who wanted to produce plays of real merit, who were anxious to try the new staging suggested by Gordon Craig without being hampered by the conventions of the professional theatre.

These people realized that drama was not intended to provide a small oasis imported from European lands, but to be an integral part of the native American scene. Little theatre and Community Theatre have a direct development relationship, though somewhat removed in time, to the call of Emerson to produce an art that might be essentially American. This development was inspired by dissatisfaction. What killed the commercial touring companies and the agencies that supported them, and indirectly created little theatres to take their place, was the fact that the tours had no relation, human or aesthetic, to the lives of the people to whom they came.

The second reason for the great impetus behind the little-theatre movement was that there were talented artists everywhere who could not find outlets in the commercial theatre.

Kenneth Macgowan has written that the history of the rebel theatre in the United States can be forced back to 1892 and the abortive Theatre of Arts and Letters (in New York City). A little less energy discovers it at work in 1906 and 1907 with the founding in Chicago of three institutions, of which two quickly passed away— the New Theatre run by Victor Mapes, the Robertson Players under

Donald Robertson, and the Hull House Players under Laura Dainty Pelham. Jane Addams, founder of Hull House, understood that bonds of race and religion are not enough to hold people together, that there must be an institution in which everyone can find expression. She wisely turned to the theatre arts to provide this satisfying activity. The years 1909-10 marked the rise and fall of the New Theatre in New York under the direction of Winthrop Ames. But for all practical purposes the true start of dramatic reform must be reckoned with in 1911, when Thomas H. Dickinson founded the Wisconsin Dramatic Society.

Thomas H. Dickinson was then a professor of English at the University of Wisconsin. In a sense he was the product of a whole development—a symbol of change, for after the Civil War there arose all over the country, thanks to an industrial boom aided by the railroads, a class of citizens with both wealth and leisure. The exclusive, lavish, Diamond Jim Brady type of entertainment pushed the idea of "people's" drama out of consciousness. The general public largely received entertainment that was quaintly naïve, sentimental, or as wildly spectacular as the circus. A mounting resentment grew which was to change ideals and make room in the American spirit for the little theatre.

A good many little theatres, arising as a result of the times, seemed not to be aware of themselves or of what they were doing. Many of them arose when friends got together and decided to start production; others were the mere playthings of arty individuals or culture grinders. A number of special groups, no matter how fine their work, failed because they could not realize that they had a place in the theatre of America. They considered themselves too inconsequential to work hard to stay alive.

ONE SIGNIFICANT
EARLY GROUP

The insurgent thinkers who motivated the Wisconsin Dramatic Society, however, seemed to be fully aware of the effect of their work. The main instigators of this unique society were Thomas H. Dickinson of Madison, Laura Sherry of Milwaukee, and Zona Gale of Portage. Miss Gale, the novelist, had not seriously written plays up to this time, although she had long had that craft in mind. Her associates said that her eyes glowed with a quality that seemed to permit her to look beyond the limits of mortal vision.

Probably because Madison was at that time a university town fermenting with ideas, a most unusual collection of people associated themselves with the Wisconsin Dramatic Society. Among the more renowned names are those of William Ellery Leonard, Thomas Wood Stevens, Percy MacKaye, Kenneth Sawyer Goodman, and Laura Sherry.

Leonard was not really a theatre man, but he was a poet, teacher, and nonconformist whose colorful personality always made him a topic of conversation. In 1912, he contributed an article to the *Drama Magazine,* "The Wisconsin Dramatic Society: An Appreciation," in which he wrote that he was so compatible with the group because, through the presentation of plays, more and more people would realize that the theatre should be and can be, not the mere refuge of the tired or worried in search of diversion, but like the art museum and the conservatory, a place where many people from all walks of life may come for study of the creative instinct of man.

Professor Dickinson's Wisconsin University English classes were exceptional in their era. This tall, thin Virginian with the soft accent, good-looking, and described as always being in "running gear," taught a dynamic course in contemporary literature. It became so popular that its reputation went beyond the campus, and after translation the course was widely used in Europe. Dickinson did not believe that the finest drama on paper was a play—it became that only when life was breathed into it by real people who acted the story.

He wished to produce plays in his classroom, but his colleagues took a conservative view of this radical kind of teaching and would not co-operate. So Dickinson and sympathetic teachers and friends, plus interested students, created the after-school-hours Wisconsin Dramatic Society.

This unique little band often worked at making a people's theatre twenty hours a day. They plunged into the whole process of play-making, including writing, and some of their earliest and greatest successes were plays written by their own members. In fact, the Wisconsin Dramatic Society was engaged in playwriting activity to a degree that caused the group to be described as a playwrights' theatre.

Some of the early productions done in Madison included *Glory of the Morning,* by Leonard; *The Neighbors,* by Zona Gale; *Dust of the Road,* by Goodman; and *In the Hospital,* by Dickinson.

Laura Sherry spread the work of the Society to Milwaukee, and because of her efforts the organization was also thought of as an experimental theatre. Milwaukee saw productions of Synge's *Riders to the Sea,* Strindberg's *The Stronger,* Shaw's *How He Lied to Her Husband,* and Laura Sherry's own play, *Just Livin'.*

Of some merit indeed was the regional drama that developed under the auspices of the Society. Dickinson promoted the regional idea by telling his followers:

"Around us people are talking a new language, not in terms of politics and science, but in terms of the simple things of living out of which a natural art comes. This we would make our language . . . the goings-on in things dramatic today have a much broader reference than merely to the stage, they refer to a society discovering itself. . . . We will be alert rather than authoritative; we would rather learn than be considered learned. We will talk about traditions, believing that in the rich human background of our history there is the soil for an art. We will talk about our people: the Norwegians,

Swedes, Germans, French, Anglo-Saxons, with transplanted instincts toward art, welded into a mass different from that of the fatherland, rich with promise. We will show that you cannot conceive of a completed society without conceiving of its theatre. . . ."

Percy MacKaye characterized the indigenous nature of the new Community Theatre movement. He wrote that the Wisconsin Idea involves the full scope of popular self-government, but that popular self-government without indigenous art forms is incapable of civilized expression. "It is the Society's policy to quicken the art of the theatre in the soil itself, through technical training of the imaginations, dramatic instincts, and latent art impulses of the people in all of their natural and local variety."

In 1915, Dickinson left Madison, moving on to the Carnegie Institute of Technology, where he joined the staff of his friend and colleague, Thomas Wood Stevens. When leadership moves away, the theatre left behind is in jeopardy, and this case was no exception. A languishing effort was made to keep the Wisconsin Dramatic Society on its feet, but it was to no avail, and the Madison branch dissolved.

IDEALISTS FOR THE IDEA

An important milestone in American Community Theatre was an organization that burst into life in an effort to develop all theatre interests into a national association. In 1910, the Drama League was born in Evanston, Illinois. Among its aims was the desire to bring better plays to small towns. This plan caught on with great rapidity, and soon there were play study-groups all over the United States preparing an intelligent audience for the coming of high-level stage drama to their local communities.

But the road shows declined, and the professional theatres did not give these lovers of drama what they sought. The Drama League decided to try something new and began an intense effort to stimulate interest in the little and Community Theatre movement, then of course still nebulous.

One of the founders of the League, Mrs. A. Starr Best, sensing the tremendous opportunity furnished by little and Community Theatres to remote communities entirely cut off from professional attractions, outlined a plan for establishing such amateur groups throughout each state. The Drama League ideals were summed up by George Bernard Shaw, who wrote: "There is much need for a spring housecleaning in the playhouse with its muck and filth, bedroom farces, and its salacious shows, silly infantile plots, and its scenes of lust and crime. The public needs something between a lecture hall and a circus. The drama must do something besides mirror the time; it must probe like a physician, feel the pulse of man today and diagnose his deepest needs and failures and desires —it must be a social drama."

After thorough and penetrating discussion in convention, the

15

League members concluded that dramatic art could not help but have healthy growth in America because it was the real reflection of mankind's desire for the fullest possible experience. They considered the theatre a natural part of the expansion of ideas, which ultimately brings tolerance and understanding. Therefore, the League resolved that its stated purposes of existence were to crowd out vicious plays by attending and commending good plays; to build up audiences for them through study courses, reading circles, and lectures; to aid in the restoration of the drama to its honorable place as the most intimate, most comprehensive, most democratic self-expression of the people both in and out of the theatre.

THE AWAKENING IN
THE UNITED STATES

By 1915 Americans seemed to be waking up to the fact that drama is not a luxury but a necessity of life, for 1915 was a banner year in the formation of little theatres. Organizations which formed strong links in the mesh of theatre across the land were established in Duluth, Cincinnati, Denver, Indianapolis, Galesburg, Ypsilanti, St. Louis, Erie, Nashville, Los Angeles, Baltimore, Cleveland, and other places too. It was the year of birth for the Neighborhood Playhouse, the Washington Square Players, the Portmanteau Players, the Provincetown Players, the Bramhall Playhouse in New York, and the Players Workshop in Chicago. These older groups have contributed immeasurably to the permanence and stability of the American Community Theatre. All were based on the premise that the artisans of the stage, in working together, themselves constituted a temporary community, which like the larger community of the audience, city or state, involves mutual understanding and common endeavor.

Sam Hume made a special contribution to Community Theatre strength in this unusual year of 1915 when he started the Arts and Crafts Theatre in Detroit. Brought to the city by the Arts and Crafts Guild to produce an open-air masque, this former Gordon Craig pupil achieved a real brilliance in his productions. Of moment was his founding, with the aid of Mrs. Edith J. R. Isaacs, of the *Theatre Arts Magazine,* which grew under the editorship of Sheldon Cheney into a periodical of international theatre communication. Later, when the Arts and Crafts Theatre dissolved, *Theatre Arts* moved to New York and was edited by Mrs. Isaacs, who was a constant supporter of the Community Theatre idea and one of its chief philosophers.

17

ROOTS IN EDUCATION

Before the First Great War the whole little-theatre program was regarded as an experiment. The amateurs were free to try all sorts of reforms in technical and acting techniques. Some of this experimentation brought obviously superior results and was at once adopted by the professional theatre. It worked both ways, however, and Thomas H. Dickinson was constantly alerting the community groups against spoiling the spontaneity of their work by imitating the professional theatre.

Numerous attacks were launched against the little theatres by newspaper critics and unhappy gossips. The movement was said to be a whim—a fad of the moment; it was accused of being the plaything of society, subscribed to by the idle rich and therefore grossly undemocratic. There were, are, and always will be a certain number of disgruntled people included in theatre groups. These persons who do not find the ultimate personal objectives which they hope for become a menace and a danger to the whole organization. This was certainly true in the second decade of this century, and perhaps from the disgruntled grew a general speculation as to the worth and direction of the movement.

Partly because of World War I, the early little theatre took only faltering steps toward becoming a worthy community enterprise. The college theatre, however, made its advent and, in a way, college theatre is the most significant factor to influence community drama.

The college theatre grew out of a merging of modern educational impulses; out of an appreciation of the value of the dramatic method in instruction, and a desire to stimulate an understanding of the world's great dramas through a differentiation between literature intended to be read and plays to be acted. It grew out of a need for playwrights, directors, and players with enough education to interpret, theatrically, aspects of life deeper and more complex than contrived situation. College theatre grew out of the necessity for giving students, intending to work professionally in the theatre, the advantage of laboratory training in association with workers in the related arts, so as to enable them to save years of effort and error in a profession in which waste is disastrously expensive. Finally, it grew out of a desire to stimulate the theatre intelligence of the American audience.

Such an inspiring idea, embracing so much, could hardly be conceived by one individual. Allowing for difference of opinion, the main share in the inception and development of college-theatre workshops must be given to George Pierce Baker of Harvard.

A legion of well-known contributors to modern theatre worked with Baker either as undergraduate or graduate students. While most of these people turned to professionalism—Broadway actually, Baker's work did much to stimulate and hearten the little-theatre pioneers. The impressive list of names includes Eugene O'Neill, Sidney Howard, Philip Barry, and Maurine Watkins, playwrights; Kenneth Macgowan, Theresa Helburn, Irving Pichel, and Sam Hume, directors; Robert Edmond Jones, Lee Simonson, and Donald Mitchell Oenslager, designers; Robert Benchley, Heywood Broun, and John Mason Brown, critics; Alexander Dean, Ester W. Bates, Sam Eliot, Jr., Alexander Drummond, Frederick H. Koch, and Allen Crafton, teachers. The inestimable labors of these artists speak for themselves.

The effect of the college theatre on the Community Theatre movement can be told through the men involved. Since Baker initiated the college theatre there have been many far-thinking teachers who have foreseen the Community Theatre as a logical adult extension of the resident academic-theatre program.

Alexander Drummond at Cornell, Frederick Koch at the University of North Carolina, Alfred Arvold at North Dakota State College, E. C. Mabie at Iowa University, Thomas Wood Stevens at Carnegie Tech, Barclay Leathem at Western Reserve, Hubert Heffner at Stanford, Glenn Hughes at the University of Washington, Allen Crafton at Kansas University, Rupel Jones at Oklahoma Uni-

versity, Samuel Selden at the University of North Carolina, Herschel
Bricker at University of Maine, Paul Baker at Baylor, Hallie Flana-
gan at Vassar and Smith—these are only a few persons of great
vision who used the college theatre to demonstrate high standards
and useful methods to the nonprofessional adult Community
Theatres.

E. C. Mabie of the University of Iowa was a guiding influence
in the creation of the American Educational Theatre Association,
and became its first president in 1936. This development was an
outgrowth of activity in the National Association of Teachers of
Speech, of which he had served as president ten years earlier.
Today, the American Educational Theatre Association contains a
Community Theatre committee, and looks forward to a full division
of Community Theatre members. Mabie believed strongly in and
made contributions to the growth of the Community Theatre, maintaining that, if it is socially significant in the lives of people, it has
an important place in education.

Alexander Drummond in New York, Alfred Arvold in North
Dakota, and Frederick H. Koch in North Carolina stimulated a
desire for drama in rural areas. They saw drama as a link between
peoples, an opening up of the enchantment of local worlds, and a
means of breaking down separations between man and his neighbor.
They saw a new kind of Community Theatre coming out of regions
served by colleges and universities. The roots of the flourishing
regional theatre conferences so important today had their beginnings in the minds of these wise college men.

A NOTE ON COURAGE

Although there is no central clearing place for factual information regarding Community Theatres, statistics gathered fairly recently show that the average Community Theatre group has been in existence thirteen years; only one in six owns its theatre, but one half of all steadily producing groups plan future buildings. The total average membership is 600, with an active participation of 150. How many groups are there? In 1952, John Beaufort, in the "Off and On Broadway" column of the *Christian Science Monitor,* said there were over 141,000. We can only suppose that he included every church, school, and fraternal group in the country. In the light of the most recent investigations it would appear that there are about 3,500 full-scale Community Theatres in the United States producing on a continuing basis. A list of approximately one thousand of these groups appears at the end of this volume.

Whatever the true number is, it is hoped that they are not pretentious, self-conscious organizations striving merely for prestige or snob appeal, and that they do not represent the lowest norm of the mediocre.

The tendency to the mediocre perhaps has something to do with what the Community Theatre has become, for studies indicate that, for better or worse, the Community Theatre of today is a sociological force as well as a cultural one. The first little theatres regarded themselves as cultural institutions, but in these days culture seems to be a by-product of a movement grown largely avocational in its objectives. A conclusion might be made that most Community Theatres try to bring good plays to their audiences, but not at the expense of the recreational function of the organization.

This puts the local director, or leader, in an uneasy position, for it is apparent that the theatre, as a community force, cannot exist amid animosity and ill will; and the ever-present problem of avoiding hurt feelings, personal slights, and other real or imagined grievances is one that must be coped with by the guiding personalities. Such hurts arise often out of the failure to attain expected goals of personal fulfillment or possibly of anticipated community receptivity. It is not suggested that directional ideals be abandoned at the insistence of enthusiastic but untrained members of the community group who wish to aim too low. Modern directors and theatre leaders who desire to be successful in a given community perhaps too often are forced to accomplish successful relationships through too elastic an approach to the local situation. How courageous a director, or group of leaders, should be is a question answerable only in direct relationship to a particular place at a particular time. Understanding of goals is cardinal.

A lack of understanding as to what the role of theatre in the community should be is the reason why there are so many attempts, far and wide across the United States, to censor Community Theatre and to censor what courageous directors and board members might like to accomplish. In Madison, Wisconsin, the Board of Education recently prohibited the Madison Theatre Guild, a Board-sponsored Community Theatre group, from doing *A Streetcar Named Desire* because it was "inappropriate" for the Board to sponsor that particular drama.

This is, of course, waving a battle flag, and as Edith Isaacs, the pioneering editor of the old *Theatre Arts Magazine,* would have said: it is the duty of Community Theatres today to tear down the false puritan art tradition, and build with the aid of art toward the puritan idea of a national life—to make American drama in the twentieth century what drama was four centuries ago, the handmaiden of the spiritual life. . . .

Nevertheless, the whole business of Community Theatre calls for tact. A Community Theatre leadership that is unwilling to move slowly, unwilling to compromise, is almost certain to head into stormy going. An aroused public, or representatives of the public, will take unto themselves the responsibility of censorship, often to the eventual shame of the community, and the failure, often, of the group.

Courage must be tempered with diplomacy to insure the maximum Community Theatre success; but a set of ideals is also absolutely essential. The right should remain with the group to perform what it pleases, but its choice ought to lie in the education and gradual raising of community standards. The shock treatment is effective but can be disastrous. People are entitled to preferences, which are determined by their own experience and the temper of the time and place in which they live. Drama seldom, if ever, originates an idea, but it is a very real power in distributing ideas. The Community Theatre may attain almost any worthy goals which it sets for itself, but it must always be aware of the local circumstances under which ideas may be most effectively distributed and received.

If the American Community Theatre is fraught with the disease of being average or mediocre or fearful, this may sometimes not be the fault of the theatre group at all, but may be the direct responsibility of the community itself. It is possible for the theatre to work upon and alter public taste. But it is equally true that the public creates its own tastes and will not, without vast physical, financial, spiritual expenditure on someone's part, change its taste, at least not for the better.

It is interesting to note the discord often arising as a result of the courage of the director to produce classic drama, for example, and the non-acceptance of such classics by the theatre group and the community. This lack of understanding, sometimes amounting to real strife, may be partly resolved by patient effort on the part of the director to integrate himself into the community instead of allowing his position to be vicarious. The wholehearted acceptance of the director by the community might do much to upgrade the choice of plays for production. The matter would seem to indicate that directors of Community Theatre need special education for their position.

How such education is to be achieved, of course, is a chief concern. The important starting point is the availability of a leader. If there is a fine local leader, the theatre program has an excellent chance of success. Unfortunately, the number of such leaders is regrettably few, and *there is no sure way to find them or to know when they will appear.* Generally, a leader will make his presence known, but not always. And when he does, he has many, many lessons to master in community and group relations.

In almost every instance where a Community Theatre has gotten off the ground, there has been an outstanding person—sometimes more than one—in the background. The best examples usually have been leaders grounded in theatre arts, but this is not always the case. Sometimes a leader is merely a civic-minded worker who has been able to carry through with a Community Theatre in an admirable way.

For the most part, leaders in Community Theatre must, to be successful, be able to do certain things. They must be able to appraise situations objectively and to take appropriate action. They must function as a communication center in the group. They must initiate or terminate action when necessary, moderate differences when they threaten to rupture communication or group action, and be able to delegate responsibility. They ought to have vision, courage, and talent.

The necessity of maintaining prestige, the avoidance of obvious enjoyment of leadership, the ability to control group emotions are all involved in the functions of objective appraisal of situations and in successful communications. And, similarly, making decisions without delay and the courage to take necessary risks are involved in initiating or terminating action. All such functions seem to work together. Objectivity, for example, is presupposed by all the others. Without it, all the other leadership functions will be disrupted. It is, in fact, a truthful measure of a leader's social sense generally.

The ability to delegate responsibility often turns on the question of the leader's security in the group, and his ability to relinquish personal control to improve the over-all operation of his organization. The sense of involvement of his followers and the rewards that go with successful activity, and indeed the entire morale of the group, are often involved. A group seems to develop best when it is challenged. Community Theatre lives or dies with the art of leadership. It survives, flourishes, goes on to something that's significant as its leaders work and think. Without leadership, Community Theatre is really nothing.

If our American theatre is lacking in the leadership it needs to give it form, it is only lacking the same quality of leadership needed by politics, religion, social action, and the other creative arts. When strong enough leaders are developed to unite the available energies and talents, the national theatre will emerge. Preparation of these leaders seems only to involve a matter of time, for the thousands of people engaged in Community Theatre work have prepared, to some degree, an understanding audience and a host of talent. With the art of theatre being widely studied in colleges, high schools, and even elementary schools, the need for leaders is immediate, and their availability must not be delayed.

It is obvious that leadership training in the whole is greatly needed in the Community Theatre program of America. Even the best leaders need help. Through a planned system of leader training for Community Theatre a whole movement would advance and might bring forward leaders who would otherwise never appear. It has been obvious for many years that some sort of national center for Community Theatre should be established so that leaders might find support, and so that Community Theatres might perhaps find leaders. The universities offering theatre courses are not, apparently, at the present time specializing enough in Community Theatre training. The lack must be filled, for as our rapidly changing social-economic patterns indicate, the theatre may be the only pause in a man's life.

THE IDEA OF COMMUNITY
THEATRE IN RETROSPECT

Thomas H. Dickinson, who stimulated the Community Theatre idea into action a half century ago, says today:

"As I think of the developments of the past decades I think I am most impressed with the extraordinary manner in which what had formerly been considered a discredited activity has been accepted into the machinery of education. Not only has it been accepted; it is now supported with funds, facilities, stages, and a place in the curriculum which would have been inconceivable a few short years ago. As one who argued for the place of the dramatic principle in education and the social order I am not sure that the pendulum has not swung too far. Education enlivened by the vital dramatic principle is one thing. Not so long ago education demanded this vitalizing infusion. But when the drama is accepted as an end in education itself, swinging the curriculum, providing the substance of 'Majors' and leading to doctorates, I am strongly disposed to think there is required a redefinition both of drama and education.

"As I observe the various dramatic courses in colleges, and the course of the theatre itself in the years since a few of us timidly tried to raise a new ensign to the winds, I am inclined to say with T. S. Eliot in one of his early poems, 'That wasn't what I meant at all.' In the colleges, in the community theatres that dot the country, the emphasis on the technical factors of staging, acting, and directing far outweighs the substance of the play itself. At the same time the quality of 'experiment' seems to have been lost. A high degree of proficiency is reached in performance. But the attempt to break the bonds of theatrical technique, to make it an agent of the expanding values and intricacies of human psychology seems to have stopped with those craftsmen who were the inspiration of a generation ago, Gordon Craig, Chekhov, Andreyev, and Pirandello.

"Amid these generalities I must stop to pay emphatic tribute to a significant outgrowth of the 'new movement of the theatre,' on the institutional side. The problem of erecting institutions with a certain amount of social and artistic integrity in the heart of the community was always a complicating factor in the visions of those who sought a more subtle and revealing artistry. In this direction something has been done. The two American Stratfords, the organization for the production of Paul Green's historical plays are examples, also the 'off-Broadway' theatres of New York. In the process of erecting standing theatres the universities are handicapped by their ever-shifting personnel.

"But I must return to the critical note. As I remember it, those who were interested in the theatre in the early days were very much alive to the fact that the trends of social and industrial life were providing a commodity hitherto unknown in a world ruled by the concept of labor alone. This commodity was 'leisure.' How was this leisure to be employed? It could be employed for the enrichment of the human spirit and the knitting of the social bond. Or it could be wasted in psychological dissociation and social disintegration. In either case drama, which is the outflow of the 'free hour,' and a filling for the vacuums of leisure, would be a decisive factor. While one must recognize and pay tribute to the valiant work done by the centers of dramatic activity throughout the country, I think the choice made by society as a whole, and by the leading figures thrown up by the dramatic movement, has been in the direction of dissolution, individual and corporate. Not to labor a point, I think we have only to compare the public position of Eugene O'Neill, the apostle of nihilism, and, for instance, Maxwell Anderson and Robert E. Sherwood, both magnificent playwrights and defenders of human stamina and corporate integrity."

Actually, whatever its current state, the Community Theatre is on solid ground, for nothing that is good theatre is alien to the human being. The more man knows about the theatre, the more man wants to know about its history, its forms and traditions, the arts which unite to serve it; and about the way it has gone and the way it is going. From personal observations in the United States and Europe, it would seem that theatre is on the increase. A vigorous and pulsing interest in all the arts is widespread at this time, and Community Theatre appears to be at the center of this upsurge.

There is an apparent hunger in the people for art; and it would seem that the theatre, traditional nursery of all the arts, is moving toward a national comprehension of its role in bringing forth from the people the best and greatest that their energy, strength, knowledge, and sense of beauty can produce—in terms of theatre art at the local level.

Recently the Humanities Division of the Ford Foundation has attempted to support this idea by making grants to ten young American playwrights and to ten producing agencies from the educational and Community Theatre to present their work. The agencies which co-operated in the plan included Community Theatres in Dallas, Erie, Omaha, San Francisco, and Tulsa. The directors of these theatres, whose subsequent interviews follow, will exert for these new scripts the finest productions of which they are capable, and will fully assist the creative development of these playwrights.

A number of contemporary local theatre leaders in widespread geographical sections of the United States and one from Britain were called upon in person and asked for opinions they might currently hold on development, playwriting, professionalism, leadership, and management in the modern Community Theatre. These conversations are presented in verbatim form in the hope that the thoughts of living, deeply concerned, conscientious directors and thinkers may be of value to the entire Community Theatre movement.

They throw the searching light of hard experience and reality on every aspect of the movement. They illustrate the best of American Community Theatre and point the way toward what it may become.

II. Conversations

Conversation with Allen Crafton

Founder of the Prairie Playhouse, 1915
Galesburg, Illinois
Then Population—22,134

THE University of Kansas has recently
opened a fine new playhouse which is the exclusive property of the
Department of Speech and Drama. The founder of the department,
and its leader for thirty-five years, is Professor Allen Crafton. He
began his work in Kansas in 1922, and made the Kansas department a pioneering venture in Middle West theatre education. Professor Crafton began his experimental work at Galesburg, Illinois,
in 1915, when he with two companions established at Galesburg
the Prairie Playhouse, first Community Theatre in a small city in
America. His conversation reveals the imagination and dedication
necessary to the solving of problems of new ventures in the beginning period of American Community Theatre.

GARD: I'm trying to sort out some of the sources of Community
Theatre in America—some of the reasons why Community Theatre
came into being, when and where it did, particularly in the first
two decades of the twentieth century. I know that you were one of
the pioneers. Do you recall any of the reasons?
CRAFTON: The reason, or reasons, back of what most of us did
in 1914–15 were: that the professional commercial theatre was
producing a second-rate fare, was getting behind the times (ignor-
ing the work of the European experimental movement), was a
closed corporation which *permitted* us laity to enter their theatre

29

upon payment of an admission price they had set. We didn't see why a theatre couldn't belong to us as well as to the "profession," and we set out to see if we were right or wrong.

GARD: You were a member of the famous Baker 47 Workshop at Harvard, weren't you?

CRAFTON: Yes. The idea for the Prairie Playhouse came from three members of Baker's 47 Workshop in Cambridge in the spring of 1915: Abby Marchant, Mark White Reed, and me. There had been no attempt to establish a little theatre in a small city. We decided to try Galesburg, Illinois—partly because it was a town of twenty-some thousand, and partly because I knew the town, having been a student at Knox College.

We arrived in Galesburg in early autumn. We had little or no money and no set plans. We collected what money we had, and borrowed a little more. The head of the English Department of the college told me, "This project is so darned crazy, I wouldn't be surprised if it succeeded."

Galesburg had voted out saloons a year or two before this. There were empty, unrented saloon buildings in a disreputable section of the business district. We could lease one, The White House Saloon, if we could locate the lease money.

We got into the place by paying a month's rent, began to clean out the filth and debris, and with the help of a carpenter began to put up a stage. I remember the building was owned by someone in Rock Island. We heard that he was in town, wanting to get the lease signed. We locked the front door, and one of us stood guard while the other two of us worked. We didn't know what we would tell the representative of the owner if he came and demanded money and signatures. . . . A friend came to our rescue and we escaped this difficulty.

GARD: What kind of fare did you give them . . . as a start?

CRAFTON: We "opened" in November with a bill of one-act plays. We gave six productions the first season. I can't remember all of them. I believe there were two one-act bills and four long plays: Gilmer's *The Edge of the World,* Shaw's *Candida,* A. E. Thomas's *Her Husband's Wife,* and Moody's *The Great Divide.* I can recall from the second year Kennedy's *The Terrible Meek* and Galsworthy's *The Pigeon.* We gave one original one-act play the first year and two the second. We held a contest and received a number of one-acts. I remember the prize was given to a teacher, Charles Mather, for his play, *The Lower Road*. At another time, a woman, the daughter of a Harvard philosophy teacher, came out and we gave one of her one-act plays. (These two were done during the second year.)

By the way, the theatre was "opened" by Mrs. A. Starr Best, President of the Drama League of America.

On the second floor of the building we fitted up a bedroom, a couple of dressing rooms, and a storage space for properties. Reed and I slept up there above the theatre.

The width of the theatre was about twenty-eight feet. This gave us a twenty-foot proscenium with four feet on each side. A physics teacher at the college brought us some rheostats, *very cheap,* which served as dimmers. We salvaged some old plywood and wrought-iron seats from the balcony of a chapel which was no longer used, and these became our theatre chairs. There was a sort of shed at the rear of the stage which had been used for storing beer kegs. It was about six feet square and became our off-stage dressing room.

GARD: Was it all volunteer work? Did you pay yourselves?

CRAFTON: The three of us took out ten dollars per week for living expenses. Total salaries, thirty dollars a week.

GARD: You couldn't make much with the small theatre.

CRAFTON: No. I forget just how many the theatre held, about one hundred. We generally ran four nights. Sometimes an organization (I recall once it was the Betas at the college) bought out a performance. We would give a group a private show for fifty dollars. In this instance, the Betas held a dinner for their dates, then came to the playhouse with them.

People were interested and helpful. For instance, there was a clever woman who was advertiser for the biggest store in town. She took over our advertising, doing a good job and charging us nothing. The daughter of the wealthiest family in town became interested, fitted up our tiny lobby with a mirror and a couple of pictures, and took over the social side of our project. She enlisted the services of a number of people (I remember particularly an ex-minister to Denmark and his wife) who served coffee and cakes between the second and third acts.

We succeeded in interesting a diverse and rather representative audience: society ladies and their reluctant husbands, a number of professional people, college faculty and students. We tried to make this everybody's theatre, and asked help from everybody and anybody. This technique was new at the time. We cast our plays from everywhere: a banker's wife, a couple of preachers, shop girls, high-school and college teachers, students—and one of our best character actors I developed from a delivery boy who began hanging around the theatre. This sort of "democratic" casting was also new.

Since we were the first small-city little theatre we got quite a bit of publicity: an article in the *New York Times;* a half page, with pictures, in *The Christian Science Monitor;* a chapter in MacKaye's *Little Theatre in the United States;* and a note in Volume I, Number 1, of *Theatre Arts Magazine.*

In late spring, 1916, a national convention of the Drama League of America was held in St. Louis. I had sent down some data as requested and I attended the convention. Two incidents remain in my memory. One was that we had the only little theatre in the country which had been completely self-supporting. And two, a short speech by Albert Halton Gilmer.

Gilmer was a professor at Tufts College. He had written a good play, *The Edge of the World,* which we had presented at the Toy Theatre in Boston and had taken on tour in Massachusetts. In the spring of '16, we gave it at the Prairie Playhouse. At the convention Gilmer said in effect, "In 1904, I was a student at Knox College and was earning my way by doing reporting on one of the local papers. One night there was a telephone call that there had been a shooting affair at the White House Saloon. I hurried over to get the story and arrived in time to see a murdered man lying on the dirty floor. I got my story and went back to the newspaper office to write it up. . . . Twelve years later my first play was produced in the old White House Saloon, which had been transformed into one of the most interesting little theatres in America."

I remember these two incidents because our little venture all at once was *something*—the leaders of the little-theatre movement had questions to ask me, and for an hour or so I was a minor celebrity!

GARD: How long did you and the others keep together as a team?

CRAFTON: Well, at the end of the first year Reed and Miss

Marchant (by the way, both of them had plays on Broadway) had had enough of the Middle West and returned to New England. I decided to carry on. I got the local Drama League to take over the theatre. The local chapter had had a spurt of interest during the previous year. So it was their theatre and I was their director. (My salary was increased to fifteen dollars per week, and I had a bookkeeper-business manager at five dollars per week. Salaries now, twenty dollars.) The second year I gave four plays. There was more interest the second year than the first. And more work. I had to direct, make scenery, do the janitor work, answer correspondence, and make an occasional speech. I also acted.

The two memories I carry from the second year are, one, the attitude of our audience toward the kind of plays we were giving. We had no pretense of "educating" anybody. We would give a good play and then a cheap, popular play. We had no sooner embarked on our second season when our audience began to ask us to do the better type rather than the cheaper sort. *They* were demanding good plays and naturally I was glad to meet their demand.

The second memory concerns several directors of little theatres in the Middle West: the Indianapolis, Maurice Brown's Chicago little theatre, Clinton Masseck's St. Louis Theatre, ours. Some of us got together for a dinner in Galesburg. I believe now we were rather sane, intelligent people who didn't have our heads in the clouds. We discussed the future possibilities for our unconventional projects and we seemed to see the future of the commercial theatre with almost prophetic accuracy. Among other matters we discussed was a "little-theatre circuit," embracing Chicago, St. Louis, and our theatre; and the interchange of plays among the three groups.

I had joined the Illinois National Guard late in March, 1917, as I was working on the set for our fifth production, *Prunella*. I received a telephone call to go over to the armory and "suit up." *Prunella* was never presented. I was in the army for over two years.

In the fall of '17, the Drama League, composed almost exclusively of women, tried to keep the Prairie Playhouse going. They didn't succeed. The project was abandoned. I never found out exactly what happened. When I returned to Galesburg in 1919, I couldn't find even a trunk that belonged to me.

I don't know whether the hundreds and thousands of us who

were interested in the amateur, noncommercial theatre in 1916
accomplished much of anything. This was a period of great enthusiasm and of *promise* rather than accomplishment. I often wonder
what would have happened if World War I hadn't come along and
put into service most of the young men who were our directors and
actors. One thing I believe is that probably the nonprofessional
theatre effort would have remained in the hands of civic or community groups, and that the "educational" theatre which began its
rise in the colleges in the twenties probably would not have developed as it did.

Conversation with Fred Burleigh
and Richard Hoover

Pittsburgh Playhouse
Pittsburgh, Pennsylvania
Population—676,806

The Pittsburgh Playhouse is one of the great "going concerns" of American Community Theatre. Its influence is flung across the entire city and reflects the free-wheeling attitude of Pittsburgh businessmen to get things done and done well. The directors of the Playhouse, Fred Burleigh and Richard Hoover, are both young men with long experience in local theatre. They respect ideas, particularly ideas which lead directly into action. Their conversation reflects their successful management.

BURLEIGH: Well, the way I feel about professionalizing the Community Theatre—right now and for years here, in Pittsburgh, we have been treated professionally by the critics. They never pull their punches, consequently our standards have had to be high for a great many years and I consider that we do rather professional work as it is. We have a professional staff to a certain extent, we have professional directors, professional scene designers, professional (by professional, I mean well-trained) people in charge of the various departments. As for the actors, though, I have a great mixture of actors, some who have had professional experience in New York, some who have trained here locally at Carnegie Tech for the theatre, and others whom I have developed myself over a period of twenty years.

35

It's pretty hard to say just what the word professional will mean, you see. I don't think I want to have a professional acting company here ever. Now, this year, as an example, the Board gave me extra money in the budget to import three professional actors from New York who would fill in as needed. Well, I found it impossible to get the type of actors who were versatile enough to fit my particular program. Right now, for instance, I am rehearsing *Teahouse of the August Moon,* which takes a very definite type. Now to do a professional production of that play I couldn't possibly afford to have professional actors from New York come and do it, you see? The next play we will be casting is *Witness for the Prosecution,* which needs an entirely different type of actor, so I feel that I can do better work at the Playhouse by using the best local talent available.

In key parts I do think it is important to have a nucleus of professional actors who will fill in as needed. But, on the whole, the general approach of the Community Theatre should always be to use the trained talent of the community in which it is existing.

GARD: You mean the volunteer talent?

BURLEIGH: Volunteer, yes. But, on the other hand, we pay our actors here something. You might be interested in this. The first time a person appears . . . with experience or not, even if he is just learning, he gets ten dollars a week for rehearsals and performances. Since we rehearse four weeks and play four weeks, this makes eighty dollars right there. Each time an actor appears, he goes up an amount—one dollar—and the top is thirty-five dollars per week. This is not bad really, because they are just working here on an avocational basis in the evening. We don't rehearse during the day at all.

GARD: Some of your volunteer actors are possibly as skilled as professionals?

BURLEIGH: Well, getting back to these avocational actors, a great many people, you know, go to New York and find that they can't make a go of the theatre there and come back here to Pittsburgh and marry, or go into business, and so on, and therefore become available to me. I have a rather large file of actors who have had a great deal of experience. I consider them professional. Although they are not paid professional salaries, they score in line with off-Broadway salaries, I suppose. I just finished doing a musical called

FRED BURLEIGH AND RICHARD HOOVER   37

Love from Judy. Well, now, you see, a young musical like that takes a definite type of person that I couldn't possibly keep on the payroll for a whole season; so getting back to your original question— I think standards, certainly, should be professional, and there should be a nucleus of a professional company in the Community Theatre.

GARD: The next question I would like to ask you is this: What kind of people attend the theatre in Pittsburgh? I mean, by the theatre, the Pittsburgh Playhouse.

BURLEIGH: Well, my policy here has always been to supplement the Nixon Theatre, which is the professional outlet for the road companies that come through. I try not to do plays that have been seen—naturally I can't get them if they will be seen—but I try to supplement their program. I see no point in doing a production of *Seven Year Itch* after it's been done at the Nixon. Consequently, I've built up an audience I feel is pretty general and they have an opportunity to see things here that the road is not giving them.

For instance, Saturday night we are opening *A View from the Bridge,* which has never been seen here in Pittsburgh. And I'm sure we have a very definite audience for it. However, there will be an audience for that play which, for example, didn't care to see *The Loud Red Patrick,* which we just finished. But we play to between 120,000 and 140,000 people per season, which I think proves that we reach rather a cross-section of the community.

GARD: Yes. And what do you charge for tickets?

BURLEIGH: This season we charge $1.75 during the week and $2.20 on Fridays and Saturdays. Next year, however, we are going to raise it to $1.95 during the week and $2.95 Fridays and Saturdays.

GARD: Do you have a paid membership?

BURLEIGH: We have a rather unique system here. We have 7,500 members. Now this is not a closed corporation, by any means. It's open to the general public. However, we do have a restaurant and cocktail lounge that work in conjunction with the theatre. A member who pays twenty-five dollars for the season is entitled to use that restaurant and the cocktail lounge and receive ten admissions to the plays, of which we usually do fourteen. The theatre is open to the general public, but those 7,500 members, you see, are a good backlog—a good base for an audience.

GARD: As far as casting is concerned, your membership actually means nothing. You can go outside?

BURLEIGH: Oh, I can use anyone. The way I do that . . . I put an ad in the paper in the fall, saying that I am having auditions, and I usually listen to about 350 to 400 people. The best people I put into my file, but anybody who has the ability can act here. It is not a closed corporation like so many of these Community Theatres are.

GARD: When was the Pittsburgh Playhouse established?

BURLEIGH: It was started by a Board of Directors in 1934. That was the time when the road was pretty dead around here and it has sprung steadily upward ever since.

GARD: And it is governed by the Board of Directors? A President?

BURLEIGH: We have a Board of Trustees and an Executive Board, and they employ me as Director and Mr. Richard Hoover as General Manager to operate the theatre.

GARD: Do you have full control over selection of plays?

BURLEIGH: Absolutely. And casting and everything.

GARD: In relation to this last question, do you have any evidence that a classic drama, a Shakespeare, for example, either increases or retards the number of people who attend your plays?

BURLEIGH: It depends on the play and the way it is done. Now, I think it is very difficult for a theatre of this kind to do the classics the way they should be done. Consequently, I don't do them very often. Unless some actor comes along who I think is particularly good for a certain leading role in a classic, I usually don't do one.

I had a very successful production of *Macbeth* several years ago. It turned out very well. But Shakespeare I don't do much because Carnegie Tech is here in the city and they do it awfully well, and I think we supplement their work, too. However, last year we did a very stylish production called *Accounting for Love,* a French farce, which was terribly successful with our audience.

GARD: Going now to the problem of the playwright in the American community—do you see any possibility of playwrights from Pittsburgh, or located in Pittsburgh, becoming a vital part of the Pittsburgh Playhouse? In other words, would you be willing to have them in residence, to encourage their work, and to produce it?

BURLEIGH: Well, since we do fourteen productions each season, it is pretty difficult, you know, to get fourteen old plays that are pretty good—so it's always been my policy to do as many new plays as I can find, but I find them very scarce.

I have one under consideration now which I will probably do at the close of the season. It's by a local author, his first play. I would say that I would do as many as three or four a season if I could find the right ones. Each year I do one if I possibly can. Last year I did Joanna Roos' *Among Ourselves.* Now I will say that it did not do well at the box office at all, but I think we have to gamble on that sort of thing. I think it's very important that we encourage new playwrights and I always read new scripts, no matter how experienced or inexperienced the playwright may be.

GARD: Very good. What are you doing to educate an audience here at the Pittsburgh Playhouse? In other words, to educate the people of Pittsburgh to a greater appreciation of living drama?

BURLEIGH: There is no active campaign to do that—it's just by constantly giving the best work that we can find and a variety of plays. I do not concentrate on one type of play, by any means. Naturally, comedy is what they like best; but on the other hand we had *Teach Me How to Cry, Loud Red Patrick, A View from the Bridge,* all following each other in the same theatre—in the small theatre. Now that's quite a variety of plays. *Teach Me How to Cry* is a very modern type of play which you would not see often; and the conventional *Bus Stop,* which had been very successful, was done in the small theatre.

GARD: I notice that you have a school of the theatre attached to the Playhouse. Is this part of an idea of educating an audience or a future audience in the community, or is it purely for the training of actors who may be of value to the Playhouse later on?

BURLEIGH: Our school is quite unique, I think. We have a two-year course. We have about forty students in our first-year course this year. The best of them will be invited back for a second season, tuition free. Those people are being trained as technicians or actors for the theatre. I don't know what the percentage will be that will ever get anywhere, but, at least, they're trying.

On the other hand, we have a large part-time program for teen-agers. They start at nine and go on up through the teens, and actually we have about 750 kids studying the theatre during the week and

on Saturdays. Then we have a dance school in connection with our
Playhouse. We train students for the musical-comedy end of it.
We also have a Playhouse Junior—the children's theatre—which
plays every Saturday during the season. The teenagers in the school
are called on to act in that or as audience, and, I think, it's developing that generation on through. I am hoping that eventually this
Playhouse Junior and the teen-age school will furnish the backbone
of our public.

GARD: Do you actively co-operate with the public schools in
Pittsburgh?

BURLEIGH: Well, yes, our children's theatre, for instance, is open
to any of the children. Sometimes the schools co-operate to the
extent of arranging transportation for us, and then our regular
theatre school gives productions. For instance, they just did *Death
of a Salesman,* and for five performances of that in our tiny studio
theatre the public schools were invited to come—a group from one
high school might come with their dramatics teacher, and to that
extent we are working with the schools. But there is no really active
campaign.

GARD: Do you have any ideas, or are you using any unique techniques, for interesting more people in the community in the Pittsburgh Playhouse? Have you changed your curtain time or anything
of that sort to suit various working groups?

BURLEIGH: We were at a Board meeting just yesterday discussing
the possibility of dropping Monday and Tuesday nights in the
theatre and adding Friday and Saturday early performances—two
performances on both of those nights. That's been tried before.
I don't think it would work here, but we'll try it. Of course, we're
not allowed to play on Sundays. We use newspaper advertising,
television, and a great deal of radio; but aside from that I don't
think there are any new techniques. I wish we could find some.

GARD: How do you see the relationship of the Pittsburgh Playhouse to other Community Theatre programs in the country?

BURLEIGH: Well, I think the very term "Community Theatre"
means that you are producing your productions for that particular
community, and things that would work in Erie or Cleveland or
Pasadena, for instance, might not work here. My problem has been
to do the best professional work on productions that I can to fit

this locality, using the talent that is available. But you should meet Dick Hoover. He's got some good ideas on all this. Would you like to meet him?

GARD: Certainly! (HOOVER *comes in presently.*) What ideas relating to Community Theatre do you feel most strongly about, Mr. Hoover?

HOOVER: Well, the thing that I feel very strongly about is the necessity of getting plays which people are interested in seeing in the Community Theatres. I mean the things they are interested in seeing far before they're interested in seeing some of the classical dramas, which I think have to come later. They're interested first in the things that they know about. And the plays that they know about are the hits that are opening on Broadway today. A play opens on Broadway, for instance, like *Auntie Mame.* Rosalind Russell's picture is on the cover of *Life,* and there are five or six pages of publicity inside. The people from the cast are on all the national television programs within a week or two after the thing opens. Every national magazine carries articles or blurbs about it. Everybody in the country knows *Auntie Mame* is the thing to see. And they all want to see it.

But these producers are sitting in New York, clutching to their bosoms property which only 1,600 people can see on a given night. My opinion is, if the plays were released on a national scale at a substantial royalty which would well pay in terms of the interest the public from coast to coast has in these hits, that theatre would really begin to exist in America again.

GARD: That's an interesting point of view. Fred, what do you think about that?

BURLEIGH: Well, I think it's a wonderful idea, but from past experience I don't know how many producers would loosen up—they are very sticky about releases. I agree with Dick—it's very important to get plays before they are tired out and worn out in New York.

HOOVER: I don't think the producers are ever going to give in on the thing unless some action is taken on it. You have your problem primarily with the play agents in New York. As you know, Community Theatres deal with Dramatists' Play Service and Samuel

French. Neither of these organizations is aggressive about getting plays. They wait until the play is presented to them to distribute.

We buy our plays from either Brandt and Brandt or French under their stock leasing, and we have been able to secure early releases on one or two plays by offering a slightly higher royalty. Money is of interest to people who are trying to get the most out of their properties.

I feel that, if an aggressive agency were set up in New York, one that even negotiated pre-production releases on the national scale, paying into the original production a sum which was not returnable, perhaps contributing $10,000 out of the play's net cost of $60,000 or $70,000, and the agency had the privilege of releasing that play nationally the minute it was opened in New York, the hits would spread from one end of the country to the other. The argument you get from the New York producers against this is, of course, that it would kill off the New York business. But I'm convinced that this isn't true. I've talked to people from all over the country and asked them about their audiences. We feel here, for instance, that the people who see New York theatre, as close as we are to New York, do not come to the Pittsburgh Playhouse. There's a snobbery about attending the Broadway theatre . . . the same thing as buying at Bergdorf-Goodman. You go to New York from Pittsburgh and buy the same merchandise and get your clothing because it's the smart and chic thing to do.

The same thing applies to the plays. We don't have people attending the Playhouse who see even one or two plays as an average in New York during the year . . . except the very few select people who are much interested in *theatre*. They would come here anyhow. And they would go anyhow to the New York theatre.

GARD: You apparently have money to spend on plays. What is your budget of operation? Mr. Hoover, how much money do you operate on during the season?

HOOVER: Our current operations are just under $300,000.

GARD: Does that include operation of your school? The whole thing?

HOOVER: Yes, except the restaurant. That's separate.

GARD: Are your buildings free of mortgage?

HOOVER: They are completely clear.

GARD: And what are your methods of operation from a business point of view? Can you describe how you operate your theatre?

HOOVER: Starting with the subscription season, which is our basic income, we have sold 8,000 subscriptions this year.

GARD: And how much are these subscriptions sold for?

HOOVER: The subscription itself is fifteen dollars, plus ten-dollar dues for the use of the restaurant. Fred was right in saying that we have 7,500 members, but in addition to the members we have a substantial number of subscribers, approximately 500, who do not care to use the restaurant. Well, while I think it's true that our restaurant is a great come-on to the theatre, we've got very good evidence that our theatre subscribers are primarily theatre subscribers, and then pay the additional ten dollars for the privilege of the use of the restaurant. I think that makes sense. The principal evidence that we have, that they're theatregoers first, is that our restaurant is completely dead when we do not have a performance going.

GARD: One might suspect it might be the other way around.

HOOVER: I remember the first time I called on Bob Breen when he was the executive director at ANTA, he said, "Pittsburgh Playhouse—oh, yes, you've got a great bar, I hear!" And we admit quite frankly that our bar is a great come-on, but it's a wonderful evening to be able to come here and park and have your dinner and go to the theatre, and perhaps have some refreshments afterward without having to chase around the city to do it. Occasionally we encounter an attitude that's unsympathetic to this method of operation, but we know, for instance, in the European theatre that it's very common to have the restaurant connected to the theatre. We think it's great and we're awfully glad we've got it.

But to go on with how we make up our budget . . . subscription forms a great chunk of our money. The twenty-five dollars times eight thousand members provides a guarantee from season to season; and, incidentally, you may be interested to know that we sell this season on April 1 of this year, effective next October 1, so we have our money available well in advance.

Then, going on from the membership subscription money, we pick up about $85,000 a year from box office for the major productions; and this is divided roughly $50,000 to $55,000 in cash box-office sales, that is, general public so to speak, and the balance of $30,000 or $35,000 is picked up from theatre parties or group sales. Then, going on beyond the theatre-performance income, we, of course, have the school tuition, which this year is approximately $35,000 for the part-time, full-time students. The children's theatre produces a very minor portion of the income. The children's theatre certainly is endowed within the operation, because the income from children's theatre is around $6,000 a year. I don't know whether Fred explained to you that we have low group rates for children because we feel that this is a very important part of our operation, and the tickets are as little as twenty-five cents to the children's theatre. The top price you pay if you come in off the street is fifty cents.

GARD: Do you ever follow the practice, as I find a good many of community groups do around the country, of selling the whole house for a particular evening to a particular group or club? Have you done that?

HOOVER: Yes, yes. We do a great deal of that. As a matter of fact, our promotion department has two people, a salesman and a clerk, who devote their full time to encouraging that.

GARD: It exposes a lot of new people to the theatre who probably never would go otherwise.

HOOVER: Well, that's true, because they come to support their own club organization, and we hope some of them like theatre well enough to come back. But to get back to *plays*. I have never been satisfied with the method in which playwrights were encouraged to write. In other words, what seems to me happens is that someone wins an award for writing a fairly decent play, and gets a grant for a play he has already written. Maybe he will, or maybe he will not, write an additional play with the award money. I am inclined to believe that playwrights are a lazy breed and I would like to see a method tried of somehow finding playwrights, or people capable of writing, and putting them on salary to write under supervision. I would think that this would be a very valuable experiment.

GARD: I've got a couple of playwrights-in-residence at Wisconsin now and I can't get anything out of them at all. One of them is a very brilliant boy. He wrote a wonderful play last year, so we gave him a full fellowship to write more. Now he's in a doldrum. Can't write a word.

HOOVER: Well, you know, a good many years ago, an aspiring writer asked Sinclair Lewis what his formula was, and he said that his formula was that he wrote every day. He admitted that a great deal of what he wrote wasn't any good at all, but he said any writer has to turn out a lot of bad stuff and cull out of it what's good. And this really is the basis of my idea about putting playwrights on salary. I mean, it's a silly thing to say, perhaps, but if you could say to a playwright, "You've got to write twenty pages of manuscript every day," I just have a feeling something would come out of it somewhere.

GARD: Well, we ought to try it sometime. Is there anything else I ought to ask Hoover about, Fred?

BURLEIGH: Well, he has a very good idea, too, about an acting fellowship scheme.

HOOVER: This idea that Fred speaks about is one that actually we hope someday to try to incorporate into our own budget. It's not an excessively expensive thing, except in terms of our present inflation. When we first worked on this plan I think we were talking of $2,000 a year for each actor the starting year. What we were kicking around was the possibility of having a pyramid acting company of people, starting with, say, ten inexperienced actors at a minimum salary, and out of that group cutting down to perhaps six in the second year, four in the third year, and two, and so on. And there is some historical background on this. I believe . . . some of the European theatres used a process of this sort in order to develop some of the finest actors for their companies. They would start with a group of students and each year eliminate some, ending up theoretically, of course, with very highly talented special people. And what we've been hoping is to work out a plan of this sort in which we pay the original group nominal salaries and then additional salaries each year to the final year, when we would hope it would be a very decent salary, and that they would then become members of a resident company.

GARD: You still have faith in this plan?

BURLEIGH: I have faith in the plan until I see the total cost of it.

HOOVER: Yes, I get worried then, too.

GARD: What is the cost of it?

HOOVER: Well, the last time we brought it up to date, I think it was something like $56,000 a year. But we revised it several times trying to get it into the budget, without ever being able to formulize it, within the scope of money available.

GARD: Has it ever been tried in the United States in Community Theatre?

HOOVER: Not to my knowledge, no. I would certainly agree with Fred McConnell at Cleveland that we need to develop our acting talent. One of our great problems, of course, is that our young people, as soon as they have had some little success here, feel the necessity of going on quickly; and certainly you can't argue with the fact that youth is one of the commodities that they have to sell. Incidentally, under this proposed plan we have talked in terms of somewhat more mature people. We were hoping that we could interest beyond-college-age people. We are very anxious to develop positions here which would enable those more mature actors to make a living.

BURLEIGH: Well, to me, the thing that has always seemed unique about the Playhouse in Pittsburgh, over any other theatre that I happen to know anything about, is the fact that it was started by, and is now operated by, the audience. All the other groups I know about . . . a director, some actors, and technicians got together and started a theatre, and maybe it was successful and maybe it wasn't. But in Pittsburgh's case, in 1934, a group got together and said, "We've got to do something about getting more theatre in Pittsburgh," and the Playhouse resulted. Our Executive Board today consists of forty-seven members, who with one or two exceptions have absolutely no knowledge or interest in the theatre, except in terms of loving theatre. They have us run the theatre for them and they don't interfere in any way at all, which is important, because I know in a lot of theatres the Boards try to pick the plays and casts and all that sort of thing.

HOOVER: Our Board of Directors seems to be completely enlightened, and I do want to say this—on our Board we've had some of the finest financial brains in Pittsburgh and this has been a tremendous help, because we couldn't begin to purchase that kind of talent for assistance in business. The fact that we now have a million-dollar investment in the plant which is free of any debt is owing to their management of our financial affairs.

Conversation with John Wray Young

Shreveport Little Theatre
Shreveport, Louisiana
Population—157,206

Shreveport, Louisiana, is a thriving city where the citizens have a deeply rooted Community Theatre, thanks to twenty-one years of the leadership of John Wray Young. Mr. Young, genial and urbane, is so sincerely dedicated to the Community Theatre as a medium for dramatic expression of the people that his presence insures enthusiastic recruits. The artistic abilities of Mrs. Young, as designer, have added full measure to the creative talent the Youngs have given to the outstanding Little Theatre of Shreveport.

Mr. and Mrs. Young, originally from the North, began their work in Shreveport because they believed it to be a privilege to create the highest standards of local drama. An ever-present regard for ideals and hard work have earned for the Youngs a place of prestige in American Community Theatre. Mr. Young is the 1959 president of the American Educational Theatre Association.

John Wray Young sees no menace to Community Theatre from the professional. He feels that playgoing is not automatic in the average person, and that there is great need to develop good audiences; that the more theatre seen, the more likely it is that America will bring into being a real national theatre.

GARD: How long has the Shreveport Little Theatre been in existence?

YOUNG: This is the final month of the thirty-fifth season.

GARD: Nineteen twenty-two, then. Who founded the Little Theatre?

YOUNG: It was organized, as so many Community Theatres have been organized, by a group of people who wanted to do something about making theatre.

GARD: They were interested in the community and the living theatre rather than in a prestige or a "club" activity?

YOUNG: Yes. It's rather interesting that the original meeting was held on the same Margaret Place on which our building now stands, one block from here, where five people met one evening in a home . . . five citizens of Shreveport, three women and two men, who decided to organize the Shreveport Little Theatre.

GARD: Do you remember some of their names?

YOUNG: Well . . . Duncan Allan Brown was one, Opal Parton was another, Julia Rogers was a third. Miss Rogers, in fact, proceeded to direct the first two seasons of the theatre, consisting of one-act plays. The first professional director was not hired until the third season.

GARD: Are any of those people now connected with the Shreveport Little Theatre?

YOUNG: No. Three of them are dead, and the other two have moved to other parts of the country.

GARD: Can you outline, very generally, the original purposes and aims of the Shreveport Little Theatre?

YOUNG: Well, it would be a question of, perhaps, assuming their purposes, because thirty-five years have gone by since their first meeting. I believe it was a feeling which prevailed generally across our country, beginning about 1912 and continuing through the decades, to try to make a better theatre than you could buy, by following certain art principles, certain standards, which were not at that time true in the commercial theatre.

GARD: Yes. Has the Shreveport group always hired a director?

YOUNG: Since the third season.

GARD: How many directors preceded you?

YOUNG: Three before me. I came here twenty-one years ago.

GARD: How was the theatre organized? Did it have a Board of Directors right from the outset?

YOUNG: No, it was a rather loosely set-up organization for the first two years, and then it was finally organized with a constitution and by-laws and a Board of Directors.

GARD: Now, is this theatre building that we are in owned by the Shreveport Little Theatre? Is it free of mortgage?

YOUNG: Yes. It was paid for before Margaret and I came in 1936, so it is owned by the members.

GARD: Does the Shreveport Little Theatre have, at the present time, any large, outstanding indebtedness?

YOUNG: No indebtedness of any kind.

GARD: Could you tell me what the general operating budget is for the Shreveport Little Theatre?

YOUNG: Yes. The budget is $25,000 per season. The money is derived from regular members, who pay eight dollars for a season of six productions, and some seventy-five patrons who pay twenty-five dollars for the season. They receive two season memberships.

GARD: What other paid staff is there beside yourself?

YOUNG: Margaret Mary Young is the designer. We have a carpenter, a secretary, and a bookkeeper.

GARD: There are five people, then, on the paid staff. And is there a children's theatre attached?

YOUNG: No. At one time we did one or two children's plays each year; but as our runs extended and we became more crowded in our plant, we gave up the children's program, which was then assumed by the Junior League of Shreveport.

GARD: Could you characterize for me the community of Shreveport as you see it from your point of view as a theatre director?

YOUNG: This has been a very interesting town in which to live for twenty-one years. When we first came here, I would say that the town was about 50 per cent old South—perhaps, a quarter Texan and a quarter Northern. Since that time the percentages have changed, until today I would say that Shreveport is one-third Southern, one-third Western, and one-third Northern. This has been due to a particular fortune in becoming the center of the natural-gas industry and the center of a great deal of the oil industry.

The offices for the leading gas corporations are located here, and that has brought into Shreveport a type of citizen which has been very desirable for Community Theatre work. They are office people, corporation people, and have made a very fine citizenry. The town has grown and the tempo of it has increased, until today Shreveport is one of the most progressive cities in the South and certainly one of the most rapidly growing.

GARD: It is to a middle-class audience that you aim your program in general?

YOUNG: Yes. We believe that a Community Theatre must be operated on a broad foundation, appealing to all the segments of a community which are capable of enjoying and participating in theatre. That doesn't include everyone. The program is designed for the family audience. It does not cater to the intellectual or to the low-brows . . . it tends to the middle ground, where the family can come to the theatre and can find their enjoyment and pleasure, and where the young people grow up and become active workers, and, in turn, their children.

GARD: Your playbill reflects this philosophy, then, I presume?

YOUNG: Yes, it reflects the wide foundation, the program directed toward the middle group of the community.

GARD: And what, in demonstration of this, has been your bill this past season?

YOUNG: We have opened with *The Bad Seed,* followed by *The Great Sebastians;* then we did *The Chalk Garden.* We turned next to a mystery by Agatha Christie called *The Mousetrap.* We followed that with *Jennie Kissed Me,* and we are concluding with an English play, which has been done in New York, called *It's Never Too Late.*

GARD: You have occasionally tried classics here, haven't you?

YOUNG: Yes. We have done some of those, but we found the audience we have does not care too much for the classics. And sometimes our college here gives free performances that satisfy the need for classics in the community dramatic program.

GARD: Do you sell a subscription type of membership or ticket?

YOUNG: We sell season memberships, which entitle the member to a reserved seat to each of six productions. We do not sell tickets outside of that. We have a closed-membership plan. This has been new in the sense that it is only five years old. It came about because we reached the point where our memberships took the capacity of our theatre, which is three hundred seats for nine performances, and we felt that, with volunteer actors and technicians, nine performances were about as many as we could do without wearing them out.

GARD: I was going to ask you about this. Do you have any problem because of the length of your run?

YOUNG: No, not at nine. If we ran eighteen, twenty, twenty-five, as some theatres do, I think we might have a problem there.

GARD: I've heard that discussed over the country—the length of run—for instance, Tulsa runs eighteen. Apparently, they have occasional difficulty holding the better actors for that many performances.

YOUNG: For the volunteer actor, who serves his community and his theatre as a fine avocation, there is a point beyond which a little of the pleasure seems to go. The excitement diminishes for the player. If it were a full-time job it would be a different matter, but volunteer actors have to make their living and take care of their families, too.

GARD: What were you doing before you came here?

YOUNG: Before we came to Shreveport we directed the Duluth Playhouse in Duluth, Minnesota. Before that we were guest directors of the Pasadena Playhouse. Prior to that we were on the faculty of the University of Iowa; and before that we had two seasons of direction of the Little Theatre of Sioux City, Iowa. This was our first theatre and we went there upon graduation from the University of Iowa.

GARD: Do you want to make any comments about any values that may be inherent in long stays as director of a Community Theatre? After all, you have been here twenty-one years.

YOUNG: I think there are many values. I think it is an essential element to growth . . . continuity of the director means a growth of purpose, a solidifying of the idea, a new respect by the community, which sees it then as a permanent part of the city structure and not as a group of people who do some plays and then get a new man.

GARD: Have you created, or caused to be created, any changes in philosophy for the Shreveport Little Theatre in the time that you have been here?

YOUNG: Yes. Like many young theatres, the Shreveport Little Theatre was pretty much a social organization. If you didn't belong to the right clubs, or know the right people, you probably didn't get on stage. The transition from that viewpoint to the broad community idea on which we exist was not easy. It took several years to

bring the change about, but we like the fact that so many of the
people we met working in this theatre twenty-one years ago are still
working with us. The few who didn't continue were those who,
I think, preferred the social-group atmosphere to the Community
Theatre climate.

GARD: Would you say that the general level for standards of
appreciation of the community, or at least a segment of it to which
you play, has risen in the last ten years?

YOUNG: Yes, I've never become too certain about the rate of
growth of appreciation in a Community Theatre audience. I think
it's destined to be a slow one. Even such a play as *The Chalk
Garden* seemed to be beyond a good part of our current audience,
and yet many in that audience have been coming to this theatre
for two or three decades. But that is also true, I think, even in New
York. They can get beyond their audience very easily up there with
a play that seems too far in one direction . . . away from the general
norms.

GARD: Now, your Board of Directors . . . is it organized as a
series of committees?

YOUNG: No. Our Board of Directors is composed of fifteen
people who are leading citizens in Shreveport. They are not chosen
because they are leading citizens, but the quality and type of people
we want on the Board demand that we choose from the people who
do most for the city. Their names appear on the Boards of the
Symphony, the Opera, the Red Cross, the Community Fund. Long
ago we gave up the idea that the members of a Board of Directors
should participate actively in the production of plays. There are
other jobs for them to do, and every member of our Board is a
worker in a field away from play production.

GARD: Well, then, how do you handle the problems of production?

YOUNG: The Theatre here—and it's true, I think, in most of the
really healthy Community Theatres—is divided squarely down the
middle. The responsibility for securing an audience, seeing to their
comfort, providing the plant, selling the memberships, running the
box office, setting up the usher corps, organizing the hostesses for
coffee service (all details, and they are vital), building expansion,
fund raising . . . all those belong to the Board of Directors. It is

their work. They have a full-time job getting these things well done. Production of the plays is the duty of the director and his staff, and once a decision is made about the play there is never any further contribution by the Board of Directors.

GARD: And as to the selection of plays, do you do that as director, or who does?

YOUNG: The selection of plays for Community Theatre is a hard and long process. We work with a play-reading committee consisting of five Board members, most of whom have served on that committee for several years. When you find someone talented in reading plays, they go on that committee at the beginning of their term. We elect our Board for three-year terms and they can serve two terms in succession, and then must go off the Board for at least one year. A good play-reading committee member is apt to serve the full six years on that committee, which means that one third of the Board of Directors is constantly reading plays. There are twenty-five readings a year. We read a minimum of one hundred to one hundred-fifty scripts a season. The scripts are suggested chiefly by the Director, because he, being an expert theatre man, is apt to know the kind of plays that he feels his theatre would like, and the kind of play it is possible to do. The committee members then serve as a sounding board for the community. Their reaction to that play, as they go through it and study it, gives a very definite idea of whether or not it is a possible choice. Once the decision is reached by mutual agreement between the committee and the Director, then the play is approved by the full Board of Directors and is sent into trial.

GARD: Now about censorship. Are you censored on anything you want to do here?

YOUNG: We censor ourselves. We have never had any difficulty with the press or any organization about any play we have done. We try to keep the plays within the range of good taste for our family audience. We cannot do *Waiting for Godot,* and if we could do it, I'm not sure I would want to do it. We cannot use excessive profanity, but I think very few plays are weakened by toning down the level of profanity from the Broadway level to a community such as ours.

GARD: Your Board of fifteen members really does all your work then, except the production of plays. Are they divided into various chairmanships, who handle different staffs?

YOUNG: Box office, ushers; but I'd better make it clear that there are a number of committee chairmen who are not Board members.

GARD: You don't contemplate anything like professionalization of your acting company here in the immediate future?

YOUNG: No. We feel, and we have noticed, that if you pay one actor you must pay all the actors. We had an arena group here called "The Courtyard Players," founded some seven years ago. They began on a volunteer basis and then started to pay one actor, then two actors. Well, of course, the secret could not be kept, and when the unpaid actors knew the others were being paid it led to the expulsion of the director. The new director came in and lasted one and one half seasons, and now that theatre is dead. And I think their great mistake was in trying to pay partially.

GARD: You have never paid anyone for acting?

YOUNG: We have never paid any actor.

GARD: What are you doing to win friends for the theatre?

YOUNG: One thing that we have been trying is an expedient and sound method for Community Theatre audience building. We invite, as theatre audiences, the drama and speech students of our various high schools to see our plays, and as we make the circuit through our five high schools we bring in these little audiences of one hundred to one hundred fifty students who are already interested in dramatic work. For many of them it's their first time in the theatre, and it gives them a taste of grown-up theatre and leads many of them to become members and workers in our group as the time goes on. It's raising a future audience and a future working group.

Public relations now ... we have found a solution there which seems to me the most satisfactory one. So many Community Theatres make the mistake of appointing a newspaperman or woman or a radio man or woman as their publicity chairman. It's already a handicap, because the loyalty of that person will go first to his employer, secondly to his theatre. The paper always looks a little askance at what is brought in because of the double interest.

We have always had our public-relations situation handled by people who did not actively work professionally as newsmen or women. But some four years ago we improved on that a bit when we went to one of our leading public-relations firms and they agreed to handle all our public-relations work as their public-service project. Other public-relations firms here do the Red Cross, the Community Fund, or the Symphony publicity as their contribution; but our firm, Robert Butcher Associates, covers and handles all releases from this theatre. On a professional basis, the items are well covered, well prepared; and they go in at the right time to the right people; and the newspapers and radio and TV stations like it very much.

GARD: Do you conduct any, what you might call, adult-education programs in the community to try to interest more people in the theatre arts?

YOUNG: Only the usual appearances that are made during the year by people of the theatre for organizations.

GARD: What is your opinion of the role that the Community Theatre ought to play in the development of the new playwright?

YOUNG: That is an old question and an old problem, as you so well know. We have done some new scripts, but antipathy comes when Community Theatres can have access to the best of new plays. In most cases, plays in the end result in the public saying, "You did *Connecticut Halloween,* when at the same time you could have given us *Death of a Salesman.* Why didn't you do that? The play you gave was not a finished script. It was not a fine play, and remember, we can only have six each year. Let the colleges do new scripts and give us plays that have been already tested through the fire of production."

What we hear sometimes, in criticism of Community Theatre, is that we do not give new playwrights a hearing. Well, it boils down to this: they don't want us to give a hearing to new plays by *established* playwrights because those plays are locked up in agents' desks in New York. They want us to produce the experimental writing of a young man or woman who thinks he or she would like to be a playwright. To produce an exercise for a Community Theatre audience who have paid their money to see a play for satisfaction, is not quite fair. If you had two auditoriums, then certainly an experimental program in new scripts and classics would be fine. We have plans for a second auditorium on the drawing board here. If we can get a quarter of a million dollars so that building may be built, we will give new scripts and classics while our main program goes on, providing the best of contemporary theatre for our audience.

GARD: Would you be willing to have a playwright-in-residence attached to the Shreveport Little Theatre?

YOUNG: We have had playwrights come when we did their plays, and it has had some satisfaction and some benefit for them. But for our audiences I don't know that there was much in it. To find a playwright who could produce even one good play a year would be remarkable, and a very happy situation. If he were not to teach playwriting but simply to write his own plays, I'm afraid his output of sound, worthy material would hardly fill much of our program on our present one-auditorium basis.

GARD: What would you say that the Shreveport Little Theatre means at the present time to the cultural life in Shreveport? Does it occupy an important position?

YOUNG: Yes, it has been stated in print and voice that the Shreveport Little Theatre is the oldest cultural organization in this city, is responsible not only for thirty-five years of good theatre in the city, but it has been an inspiration for the beginning of many other cultural activities. Our Symphony is nine years old, our Opera Association is seven years old, and people of these organizations have said that they couldn't get any place if the Shreveport Little Theatre hadn't laid the groundwork, hadn't established the idea in the collective mind that cultural projects are an important part of our civic pattern.

GARD: Has anyone ever considered an integration of these activities . . . music, art, and theatre?

YOUNG: That has been talked about, but nothing definite has been done.

GARD: Let yourself dream a moment of what the Community Theatre might mean for America, in the greatest sense.

YOUNG: Well, it already means a great deal. There's an amazing amount of sound activity, a great appreciation, a wide enthusiasm across the land, but you have to go to the cities to realize the extent of that interest and enthusiasm. What I have been working on is to establish liaison in the Community Theatre field, to get it pulled together where we can spare the learning of old problems by new organizations . . . where the solutions that have been found can be passed on . . . where the strength of organization can come to the

Community Theatres which, after all, represent the top citizens of their communities in towns and villages across our land.

I believe that someday we will get the Community Theatres into a strong, honest, integrated organization; and when that happens, it will be a great and important step forward. Although the force is there already, it just is not widely apparent in many cases. But I think, from my personal viewpoint, it would be most important to work toward the establishing of communication lines, such as: to encourage the organization of state Community Theatre groups; to give assistance to the already organized regional theatre conferences which have come so far in so short a time; to make the Americans working at play production across the land aware of what is happening to other people in other organizations and to begin to build bridges of communication between groups; to exchange information; to send visiting experts, particularly to the young groups that need help; to establish patterns of procedure, so that we would not continue to see hundreds of new groups fumbling along, getting lost, and only a few surviving.

Conversation with Eric Salmon

Shrewsbury Drama Group
Shrewsbury, England
Population—60,000

The movement described by Professor Crafton was also gaining ground in Britain, and has continued as a healthy, locally rooted theatre expression to the present time. Mr. Eric Salmon, young British producer and county drama adviser, gives in the description to follow the development of the whole idea of Community Theatre as it has grown in the British Isles.

Eric Salmon has been Shropshire County Drama Advisor and Director of the Shrewsbury Drama Group for ten years. The appeal of this agricultural community lured the tall, energetic man with an actor's face from college teaching. He speaks rapidly and interestingly of his all-day, all-night labors to bring good drama to Shrewsbury and the smaller county towns.

Mr. Salmon believes that people should have the opportunity to see the very best plays, that somehow they must be led from the false idea that only commercial successes are worth while. His first production in Shropshire was *The Insect Comedy,* by the Capek brothers, and this was undertaken with the full realization that it might make him seem foolish if it failed. The risk paid off—newspaper reviews were favorable, and the audience applauded the show. Mr. Salmon proved that to hold to the ideal of doing only good or great plays has rich reward.

These community productions have been acted entirely in the school buildings by local persons whose daytime work ranged from garage employee to owner of the largest department store. After productions were successfully under way, the Shrewsbury Drama Guild was established solely to encourage living theatre. This they did by sponsoring the producing group and by booking worth-while outside attractions. Play-reading groups sprang up throughout the county, and drama has indeed earned a prominent place in the people's lives.

Mr. Salmon's philosophy behind this work is that it is important in this atmosphere in which we live to have "beauty for beauty's sake." He agrees that few theatre people can say this without self-consciousness, but that there is real need to do something about it *now*.

GARD: How long has Community Theatre been in existence in England?

SALMON: "Community Theatre," as a term, has not been much used in England; the usual title would be "amateur theatre," or "nonprofessional theatre" if the speaker is pedantic. Whatever it is called, as a movement, it has existed as a consciously formed and recognizable entity for a relatively short time, perhaps only fifty years or so. There have, of course, been groups of amateur actors for vastly longer than this: the miracle and mystery plays of medieval times were played by amateur actors, and the early Elizabethan dramatists wrote their curious creaking plays for companies of schoolboys or companies of noblemen at play. And in more recent times, the provinces of England, towns distant from the capital, have had theatre of one sort or another, sometimes amateur, sometimes professional, supported (or not, as the case may be) by the community and in some sense serving the community.

William Poel, the great reviver of interest in the vitality of Shakespeare's work, tells a quaint story of his early life as an actor with a company of touring players working in the English countryside. But Community Theatre is a new idea, the idea of linking a theatre closely with the life of the area from which it springs, and of using that theatre not merely as a place to while away the long age of three hours between after-supper and bedtime but as a lively, challenging, and provocative art form.

GARD: What sort of people have been the leaders of the Community Theatre movement in England?

SALMON: Two parallel lines of development can be discerned in Britain: the work respectively of amateur actors and directors on the one hand, and of professional theatre people on the other. But at the outset a common factor should be noted: whether amateurs or professionals, the only people whose work has been significant have been those who lived only for theatre and were almost prepared to die for it. They have never been professionals who thought it was a way of making a living. They have never been amateurs who thought it a pleasant way of spending their spare time or a good way of showing off; they have never been casual; they have never been cautious. On the whole, they have never really been community-minded, either. They have been people who believed with a deep, unshakable, and often inexpressible belief that the world's great minds should mingle with the commonest sort of people, even if the particular minds in question happened to express themselves in the form of dialogues and dramas. They believe that the mighty words of the world's great plays should ring in our ears even as we tread the everyday street of life, that the laughter should roll and the tears should run to lift people above the commonplace.

They have never, these pioneers of Community Theatre, been too anxious to please; they never tried to consider what the paying customer wanted: they gave him, because they couldn't help themselves, what they thought he *needed*. And the paying customer, often in sufficient numbers to pay the bills, recognized their honesty, their purpose, and their worth, and went on paying.

GARD: Won't you tell me about the early Community Theatre efforts in your country?

SALMON: One of the very early professional experiments was that of Miss A. E. F. Horniman at the Gaiety Theatre in Manchester. She was a woman of independent means who assembled around her a group of young actors and actresses in the period immediately preceding the First World War, and in her Gaiety, long since a cinema, proceeded to produce for the phlegmatic audiences of industrial south Lancashire the early plays of Shaw, the disturbing dramas which came from the Norwegian's gloomy, mighty hand, and similar unlikely fare. She also did another thing: she founded by accident a school of dramatic writing ("school" in the sense of style, not a place of instruction). This became known as the Northern School of playwrights.

Like the Irish theatre movement, it was all over quickly; like the Irish, too, its first expression was its most splendid; and like the Irish movement, it expressed the exact spirit of a particular time and particular place so accurately, so vividly, that the truth of the expressing spread itself out into other times and places.

These plays were spare, stripped, hard-knuckled realism; angular as the country and people who inspired them; and, like them, honest, spirited, and warm-hearted. They were, too, *town* plays: neither countryside nor city pieces, but town plays, the smaller Lancashire cotton towns, ugly, fairly dirty, and boundlessly energetic —and with the poetry of honesty and common sense gleaming in every line.

In Birmingham, Barry Jackson also had a writer linked closely to his theatre—John Drinkwater. The Birmingham Repertory Theatre, still one of the best of English provincial theatres and one of the most attractive, was opened in 1911. Drinkwater's *Abraham Lincoln* was first played there, as were *Mary Stuart* and *Oliver Cromwell*.

These two, and some others like them (William Armstron at the Liverpool Playhouse, for example), were true Community Theatres. They never used amateur actors but they really *belonged* to their own communities, not by virtue of financial ties, but because they created standards which otherwise would not have been there and because they won the hearts of local people and the constant and ready support of local people in doing so.

GARD: Inasmuch as those were all professional groups, what about the completely amateur organizations? How did these come to get started, where did they operate, and what kind of drama did they produce?

SALMON: In the years just after the First World War, a similar movement began to develop in the amateur theatre. Amateur dramatic societies had existed for a long time, performing politely in the local town hall two or three times a year, trimmed out with bouquets and boxes of chocolates on the final night (inevitably a Saturday) handed over the footlights to the leading lady who received them will ill-simulated surprise. Such activity was innocuous and doubtless of great social value; it was artistically worthless and still is. But the new amateur movement was an entirely different breed of animal. These people really meant business: they worked and slaved at the thing. It became a dragon which consumed every moment of spare time. They taught themselves to act, taught themselves to direct plays; they employed fantastic ingenuity to produce lighting effects of quite startling beauty and usefulness with equipment that would make a professional stage electrician weep. They built their own theatres; they rehearsed and rehearsed and rehearsed. Their labors were increasing and their energy was inexhaustible.

And from this strange ferment came theatres like Nugent Monck's Maddermarket at Norwich, the Questors at Ealing, the Highbury Little Theatre at Sutton Coldfield in Warwickshire, the Unnamed Society of Manchester, the Crescent at Birmingham, the People's Theatre at Newcastle-on-Tyne, the Civic at Bradford, the Halifax Thespians Society, and a score of others. In more recent years, such theatres as these have been organized into the Little Theatre Guild of Great Britain, a federation reserved for those organizations which possess their own premises.

The Halifax Thespians have converted a former Methodist chapel; the Unnamed Society have taken over one of the huge galleries of the Whitworth Art Gallery on Oxford Road, Manchester; the members of the Highbury Little Theatre built their own theatre, brick by brick. The Questors, more ambitious than the rest, have embarked on an extensive building program for which Dr. Richard Southern prepared designs and for which money is being raised by public subscription.

Though it is not possible to generalize about a creative art whose life-book is variety of expression, it is true in the main to say that the policy of all the above-mentioned societies has always been to present only plays of great quality and merit, or plays of a rare sort or of unusual interest. "Theatre of the more intelligent sort," says the constitution of the Halifax society.

Some of them are more esoteric in their choice of material than others, but all are dedicated to the idea that an audience *likes* to be challenged, prefers to be wakened rather than rocked to sleep: not all audiences, of course, nor all of every audience, but enough to make the effort worth while, enough to cause us to go on hoping for humanity. A significant factor is the devotion of this kind of theatre to poetic drama, especially the new poetic drama. *The Ascent of F 6* swept through every one of these little playhouses; so did *Murder in the Cathedral* and *Happy as Larry*. Christopher Fry was hailed by them, and all his plays, from *Boy with a Cart* to *Sleep of Prisoners*, were joyously grabbed and performed, even the little-known ones, like *Thor, with Angels* and *The First Born*. Minor poet-dramatists such as Ronald Duncan, Gilbert Horrobin, and Henry Treece had first performances given by these amateur theatres. Norman Nicholsen, whose first play, *The Old Man of the Mountains,* was written at the insistence of E. Martin Browne for his season of plays by poets at the little Mercury Theatre in London, wrote his second play, *Prophesy to the Wind,* in response to a request and specific commission by the Little Theatre Guild.

Since the beginning of the century the work of smaller units has grown and developed, too. Alongside the larger and better-known amateur theatres that were working in their own premises, have grown up many groups, especially in smaller towns, that have little hope of ever owning a theatre, however humble, but whose work is yet significant and stimulating. Operating in the halls of public buildings and schools, these societies yet contrive to mount great and exciting plays in an exciting way.

GARD: What is the British Drama League doing at this time to promote the Community Theatre?

SALMON: The British Drama League has an affiliation membership of several thousands. Not all of these do good works, of course. Many are still devoted to imitating the commercial stage of Shaftesbury Avenue, pathetically aping popular entertainment and wondering why they aren't popular. But *some* do good work; some really are a community expression of real theatrical worth.

The British Drama League has done in the past twenty-five years enormous good in this field of nonprofessional drama. It has organized all sorts of training courses, from one day to three months in length; it has provided a valuable library service of plays and books about the theatre; it has published a quarterly magazine of high quality. Perhaps its most remarkable piece of work has been the annual organizing of the Festival of Community Drama. This is an immense competition for performance by local groups from all over

England, Wales, and Scotland of one-act plays. It begins in November or December at local level, with some ten or twelve groups presenting plays in village halls, town halls, school halls all over the country. The best are selected by skilled adjudicators to go forward to a larger competition in the Area Final, then to the Divisional Final and then, in May, to the Scala Theatre in London for the British Isles Final. One sees in this competition, year by year, hundreds of worthless one-act plays badly performed; but one also sees performances that would not disgrace the best professional stages, of plays by Shaw, Synge, Barrie, Chekhov, Maeterlinck, and many others. There is a perennial argument in England about whether drama should be made the subject of competition, whether art and competition are not mutually incompatible, and it is certainly true that some of the Festival's occasions are characterized more by the spirit of cutthroat rivalry than by any sense of brotherhood of artistic endeavor. Nevertheless, there is much to be said on both sides, and the plain fact which cannot be gainsaid is that this Festival Competition has, during the last twenty years, done much not only to raise physical standards of presentation but also to make many communities aware of the live stage which otherwise have remained ignorant of it and to increase the seriousness of purpose of many amateur actors and directors. A special feature of this British Drama League Festival, which has now also spread to other Festival organizations, is the public adjudicator. This has become the accepted climax of the whole occasion. The adjudicator, usually now a member of the Guild of Drama Adjudicators, often comes from the other end of the country to do this work. At the end of each evening's performances he takes the stage and talks about the plays for some forty minutes before announcing his placing of them in the competition. He is also required, usually, to let the competing team have, afterward, a written report about their play. Wise adjudicators concentrate on the worth of the play at least as much as the technical proficiency of the performers: thus, audience taste is gradually trained and raised as well as performers' craftsmanship improved.

There is a great deal of amateur drama activity in England, some of it genuine Community Theatre. Some of it is excellent, exciting, adventurous, and a real power and formative influence in English theatre as a whole; some of it is good, honest workmanship; some of it is nonsense. The chief lack, now as ever, is a large enough number of directors—producers, the English call them—with real vision, real courage, and real devotion, men who believe the theatre is not just pleasant but also important, men who combine knowledge and love of great plays with the ability to make use of people for artistic purposes and, in doing so, win the loyalty of those people. More plays are needed, too, especially plays which take up in a big and challenging way the big and challenging questions of our day— questions of race, color, creed, and belief. England still has, in its smaller playhouses as in its larger, too many men who say, "We must avoid controversial topics; *somebody* mightn't like them." Drama avoid controversy? Surely a contradiction in terms.

Conversation with Jack Higgins

Theatres of the Chicago Park District
Chicago, Illinois
Population—3,620,962

Jack is Supervisor of Drama for the entire Chicago Park District. A former musician, he got the drama job during the depression years of the 1930's and has built it, with sympathetic aid from his administrators, into a flourishing program including twenty-one theatres. He is easygoing on the outside, tall, gray, pipe-smoking. He houses scenery, properties, and conducts a costume shop for the District in the old carriage house of the Columbian Exposition of 1893. This immense, round building on South 57th Street holds the outstanding collection of theatrical odds and ends in the Middle West. From it trucks carry necessary materials to all the theatre centers of the Park District; but Jack Higgins himself is the nerve center, the guiding director for it all. His dialogue is rapid, direct.

Chicago is, as everyone knows, a fascinating study for both the scholar and the mere interested observer. "Why," runs the invariable question, "is Chicago so backward culturally?" So far nobody has been able to produce a first-rate answer. It is apparent that many great movements have begun in Chicago. Take, for instance, the symbolization of the Auditorium Theatre, which for fifty years was the center of great music and drama in those days when Chicago was recognized as the cultural center of the Middle West. The good things always seem to go away.

The city is Big, but it is second Big. It seems forever losing out in its struggle for talent with New York or Los Angeles. Chicagoans

66

themselves, perhaps, are outstanding victims, nationally, of a tremendous inferiority complex. Perhaps they themselves consider Chicago nowadays second-rate culturally, and for that reason do not think it worth the effort to compete with New York.

Communications are excellent. It's easy to get to town from the suburbs. But Chicagoans will let a good attempt to establish a professional repertory theatre perish in a year. A few road shows do modestly well if they have first been successful in New York.

Dallas, Houston, Cleveland, Los Angeles, almost any of them is better off than Chicago, for they are not second best. It's a terrific burden and perhaps a terrible stigma. Perhaps when Los Angeles overcomes Chicago population-wise, Chicago will lose its inferiority, become more than a crossroads or a burbling, howling railhead and an air terminal.

Chicago is perhaps the most interesting city in America and it has least realized itself in the last three decades. Fifty years or less ago, Chicago was a city of green promise for all of American art. Jack Higgins is working at the problem, in the proper way, from the roots and the inside, from the South Side and the North Side, with Negro and white.

GARD: How did the Chicago Park District get interested in Community Theatre for adults? Has it been a program that's existed for a long while?

HIGGINS: I came with the District in 1933, and at that time we had—it was before our so-called consolidation—twenty-one separate communities that had their own park setups. And then, of course, when Mr. Robert Dunham came in, he had that dream of consolidating, so we are now consolidated; and the result is that's why we have these one hundred and sixty-four parks. It has been a big saving for the taxpayers and also the bondholders. It's all under one head now.

But you must also remember the Chicago Park District is a city within a city. We are divorced from the City of Chicago, inasmuch as we have our own police department, our own law department, all various departments and divisions, our boulevards, and our network of parks, city-wide, that are absolutely apart from the city. It's hard for people to understand our system, for when we are in our own back yard—I mean the District—we must stay in our own back yard.

GARD: You are sole drama director for the Chicago Park District, are you not?

HIGGINS: Let us say I'm the supervisor of drama, to this extent, that I help my staff. I really haven't any time to do any directing at all.

GARD: Do I understand that your staff directs the plays at all fifteen Community Theatres?

HIGGINS: Not all of them. We have two groups that have volunteer directors; but those directors act according to Park policy, follow all the rules and regulations that the Park has, and they are not out to make money.

The thing is that all the monies that are accepted in the Park must go through the Park supervisor who runs that Park.

GARD: How many people do you have on your drama staff?

HIGGINS: We have seventeen full-time drama instructors and, besides these seventeen instructors, I have twelve hourly people . . . people who are mostly students working their way through school.

GARD: How does the wintertime program, in administration, differ from the summer program?

HIGGINS: We have a tremendous summer program known as day camps. Three or four instructors or directors, whom I have carrying the summer theatre program, carry on normally, just as they do in the wintertime. But the balance of my people go to the day camps and are supposed to have a change of routine.

GARD: Are these summer theatre performances, conducted in arena style on the lake front, well attended by the public?

HIGGINS: You may be surprised, but many a time I've turned away anywhere from fifty to one hundred people; standing room only.

GARD: I was asking you about the significance of Community Theatre in the total cultural life of Chicago. Do you think it has any significance?

HIGGINS: I'm afraid it's a little small at this time. We can't give it a yardstick measure for this reason: television, you know, robs us of so many people. The younger generation is not familiar with live shows, and the prices are high. We're trying awfully hard in our field to establish these large audiences and get to these people, but it's not only the Park District. City-wide and within our Chicagoland, we have something like twenty-five or thirty other big community cultural affairs. We find that on the border of our city limits we get more support for these things than we do in the local areas.

However, there is one thing that is amazing. The Negroes have come along very, very well. You'd be surprised at the high type of work they are doing and at the crowds that turn out for their plays.

GARD: Are some of these fifteen Community Theatres Negro groups?

HIGGINS: Yes, and I have five Negroes working on my staff.

GARD: What do you see as the potential for Chicago? Speaking from the Community Theatre point of view, what is the participation of people in theatre programs and the receptivity of such programs by the people of Chicago? What do you foresee happening in the next five or ten years?

HIGGINS: There's no reason why the Park District shouldn't have at least three real theatres, North, West, and South. Surveys show that the public schools have their theatres; the Jewish Institute on the West Side has theirs; the parochial school systems have their theatres with border lights and switchboards; private institutions have them, like the Goodman, which is on Park property, incidentally.

But the Park District has not one dished floor, with fly loft and grid, not one first-class theatre with facilities which will entice people into it.

GARD: Do you have any idea how the ordinary citizen's attitude toward living theatre might be changed by putting the theatre in different kinds of locations, or changing the times of theatre production?

HIGGINS: I've noticed a good many theatres are running Sundays, like Northwestern's, which has a four-o'clock performance. In our case, a good many times we start at seven, or seven-thirty. Gives people a longer evening.

GARD: As people get more leisure something certainly has to be done to change the times of doing things. The old patterns don't seem to work, do they?

HIGGINS: I'm afraid not. It must be remembered that we have both passive recreation and active recreation. We can't overlook the passive or audience participation end of it. The desires of the spectators, in the theatre arts, are more important, if we're to raise standards and increase interest in theatre, than the problems of the participants—the volunteer actors.

Conversation with Newell Tarrant

Erie Playhouse, Erie, Pennsylvania
Population—130,802

On a snowy morning in March a visit was paid to the Erie Playhouse, Erie, Pennsylvania. This is one of the few completely professional Community Theatres in America. It is located in the heart of downtown Erie and is a separate theatre building. Its director, Newell Tarrant, is decisive, stocky, rapid-speaking.

Here, talk was sought particularly regarding the professional actor in Community Theatre. Ideas were preconceived when Erie was visited. For instance, it seemed doubtful that the great body and bulk of Community Theatres in America will have completely professional acting companies. The voluntary aspect is far too vital, too important, and too practical; it is the very lifeblood and reason for being of many flourishing groups. Indeed, in pure financial terms, professional theatres would find themselves in a very serious condition if they attempted to accomplish the range of production done by volunteer companies.

Where a strong hobby or self-expression motive is more vital than art purpose, Community Theatre will most likely remain an amateur organization, though it may have a paid director. Paid directors seem to raise the standards of productions, although they do not necessarily solve the question of better play choice and community education in drama.

A 1957 Community Theatre study in Wisconsin revealed that only a smattering of modern plays written before 1947 were produced, and among these only a few plays of a serious nature and

71

extremely few classics. This expected news is revelatory of the fact that the recreation motive is extremely strong in Wisconsin, as it is elsewhere, and that there are still very few paid directors in the Community Theatre in the state. In those places—Milwaukee, Green Bay, Kenosha, Sheboygan, and Madison notably—where there are paid directors, the levels of play choice were higher but revealed, in most instances, a distinct tendency toward pandering to lower levels of public taste. Fearlessness and courage to try unusual or off-beat plays seem to be purely a matter of individual personal taste and drive in the individual director and the group itself.

Insofar as community professional acting companies are concerned, they are emerging in a limited number of larger places such as Erie, Dallas, Milwaukee, San Francisco, Cleveland, Pittsburgh, and Houston. It seems that this is a movement that should be encouraged in centers where there is audience enough and scope enough for the recreative and professional point of view to exist side by side. This is possible in San Francisco, for example, where there are several high-quality, completely volunteer theatres doing excellent work and able to draw excellent audiences even while the professional Actors Workshop productions are playing to excellent houses.

If there is a demand for an increasing number of performances, then the paid actor becomes a must. The volunteer cannot often afford to sacrifice the time that is necessary to play more than approximately twenty performances.

It is apparently possible, as many Community Theatres have demonstrated, to mix the professional actor with the amateur. Opponents of this practice claim that the level between the professional and the amateur is so discernible that it destroys the unity of the play. But others point out that the levels are equally apparent between the star performer in New York and the other professionals in the cast. The "star system," where it has been tried over a period of time by professional Community Theatres, has generally been found to contain more drawbacks than assets. The quality of stars available at any one time varies tremendously, and it has been found that the variance in quality of star performers has itself been a hindrance. Everybody knows that the reputations of most so-called "stars" have been overinflated, and that most of them can't act.

Without question, the Community Theatre can both benefit and suffer from the professional. There is a very real danger, when a theatre professionalizes, of siphoning off some of the devoted community interest. The average Community Theatre has been organized by people who want to act and want to participate. When their opportunity to act is lessened, they may quit. It is very important to any professional theatre, especially of the smaller kind, that there be provision made for extensive use of superior local talent. It should be an honor to develop in the craft to a professional level.

There are an increasing number of highly qualified competent amateur actors who are in many instances as skilled as so-called "professionals." Such persons are the backbone of many of the most successful groups, though the frequency with which these outstanding amateurs play is a major consideration. For purposes of "democracy," leading parts are given to favored performers perhaps only once in a season.

Community Theatre might eventually, at least in larger centers, offer wide employment to actors, particularly if the actors themselves are based in the home community. The concept or motive of Community Theatre is pre-eminently local, and professionals can be localized. Itinerant actors are not a satisfactory answer any more than a mere series of professional touring companies would be the complete answer.

So confirmation of theories was sought at Erie with Newell Tarrant.

GARD: The Erie Pennsylvania Playhouse has been in existence since the spring of 1916. The Playhouse was founded, wasn't it, by Henry Vincent, who was a yachtsman and leader of an orchestra here?

TARRANT: He was a cultural leader here in the community, a very accomplished musician, and he became interested in theatre. He saw to it that there was theatre in Erie.

GARD: So I suppose you could have expected the early years of the Playhouse in Erie to have been like other early American Community Theatres . . . a sort of upper-crust activity.

TARRANT: Yes, I would say that the history of the Erie Playhouse is a direct parallel with the history of the Community Theatre movement in America, developing right on through to what I think should be the ultimate goal of them all . . . professionalization.

GARD: I'd like to hold off pursuit of professionalization for a moment. You mentioned earlier this morning that the people who had a lot to do with the Playhouse were of a particularly independent breed.

TARRANT: Yes, that's true. There has been a great deal of pride in rugged individualism to a point possibly of folly, in that the Playhouse has never asked for help from any national organizations. It never asked for help from anyone; in fact, it is the only theatre that I know of at the community level in the United States that has not accepted one dime of support other than that which comes in on membership dues. In fact, a couple of years ago a very charming person in the community died, and a friend of hers sent, instead of flowers, a check for twenty-five dollars to be passed on to her favorite cultural activity. The twenty-five dollars were sent to the Playhouse.

In a Board meeting that ensued there was something like thirty minutes of discussion as to just how, within the framework of our policy, we could accept this gift of twenty-five dollars.

GARD: Is the Erie Playhouse fairly solvent financially right now?

TARRANT: Well, we have been going broke for forty years. We have a building that I would say is valued at anywhere from $80,000 to $150,000. Our only indebtedness is a mortgage, which has been hacked down through the years, and now is between $12,000 and $13,000.

GARD: What do you think the Erie Playhouse means to the community of Erie?

TARRANT: Of course, I'm prejudiced. I think it means a great deal. I have directed in Community Theatres almost all over the United States and I have seen the effect on community life in various places, and . . . but first let's see what Erie is.

Erie is a small industrial city of about 138,000 people. It is made up largely of people who were originally brought in as low-priced labor, cheap labor, people who were brought over from other countries to work in the industrial area before unionization, before the rights of man were considered to be very much. Now Erie has not entirely assimilated this aspect of her population. But, in spite of it (or perhaps because of it), Erie has a very vital and active philharmonic symphony with a full-time conductor. Erie has one of the very few professional Community Theatres in the United States. The Playhouse is the oldest of the cultural organizations, and when you consider, in a city of 138,000 people, we have affiliated with the Playhouse 5,500 families, not 5,500 individuals, but families, there must be some impact on the community.

I would say that our audiences are about 80 per cent in the lower middle class as far as income level, and what might be called educational level, of the community. Only 20 per cent come from what might be called the upper strata.

GARD: You seem to imply that the audience may not have had a great background in knowledge of the living theatre.

TARRANT: The only background most of them have is the Playhouse in Erie. I don't mean that this is one of those theatres of the people, these so-called "propaganda" theatres. This is not true; but as a Community Theatre, and I have directed in many cities in the United States, this one has the most homogeneous audience.

GARD: What kind of plays do you have to present to this audience which is 80 per cent of the American working class?

TARRANT: I wish it were possible to generalize. We've done everything. I'd say at the very top was *I Remember Mama* and *Taming of the Shrew*. And right along with them are *Dear Ruth*, *Harvey, Mister Roberts, Stalag 17*. What does that tell you? If a show is well written from the standpoint of theatre—not always literature—and if it is well done, and if there is some association with the Broadway theatre that can be publicized, it sells.

GARD: Ever tried Ibsen here in Erie?

TARRANT: Well, Ibsen was my thesis when I got my master's degree; but I was warned by the Board of Directors when I came to town that Mr. Ibsen, the last time he played here, drew an astounding audience of twenty-five people, and so I have preferred to do Shaw, Shakespeare, and others, rather than bring out one of my favorite playwrights.

GARD: Do you use any special public-relations approaches to interest people in the Playhouse?

TARRANT: We use any honorable approach that we can think of. For example, we have coming up a production of *Bus Stop*. Now we know this show is no great literary achievement, and yet it is a popular show from Broadway. We are doing it in the Lenten season, a time when business is off in most theatres.

GARD: By the way, is Erie predominantly Catholic?

TARRANT: Predominantly Catholic, yes. The Playhouse does not allow any organization to tell it how to operate, but we find that when we are operating for a public, it is utterly foolish not to give that public something that is in line with their moral principles. So we try to comply to whatever extent we can, without destroying the integrity of our production.

Well, anyway, with *Bus Stop,* we have a little gimmick going now with the bus company. Next week, in the front of every bus will be a sign about twenty-two by thirty-five inches that will advertise *Bus Stop,* and in small print will be stated that a free ticket to this play will be given to every purchaser of a two-dollar bus coupon. This is in co-operation with the bus company. It gives them advertising, and it's going to fill up some empty seats during Lent. So we don't mind going sensational.

GARD: Do you ever do anything with plays of religious content? Say, would it be possible for you to produce such a play successfully during this Lenten season?

TARRANT: Well, we have found that the Lenten season is the time of the year to do shows that people of very strict religious conviction might be offended by. Nothing will bring out a person who is dedicated not to go out during Lent. If you have a sensational show that's a little bit bawdy . . . a lot of people forget their religion and come. I tried with some friends of mine of the Catholic Church to think of shows that would be especially acceptable to a Catholic audience and to any very strict Christian audience during Lent. And the answer was . . . if it's a Passion play—maybe. But the theatre is just out during Lent for the "devout." I say "devout" in quotes.

GARD: Do you do the ordinary kind of newspaper and radio publicity for each one of your shows?

TARRANT: No, we have found that the media in this town are extremely co-operative. The radio stations go all out for us and give us tremendous co-operation. The TV stations to a little less degree because their time is so much more expensive, but they have never really denied us anything. I think our reputation is sufficiently good in the community that any time we want to take our profes-

sional company down to a TV station and do an excerpt from a
show the time is available for us, but it costs us money to do that.

GARD: You have to pay for it? They don't donate the time?

TARRANT: They donate the time, yes, but we have to provide the
talent; and when you are paying salaries, that's the thing to watch.

GARD: Now, let's get at this business of the professionalization
of the Community Theatre. I take it, since the Erie Playhouse is—
what—one of a half dozen professional Community Theatres?

TARRANT: Cleveland is the daddy of them all, and Margo Jones
Theatre in Dallas is making quite a record, and the Alley down in
Houston, and the Fred Miller in Milwaukee, and a few more. But
the only two in the United States which have survived for· a long
time have been Cleveland and Erie.

GARD: Now, I take it that you must think that professionalism
of the Community Theatre is a good thing?

TARRANT: I'm thoroughly sold on it. I came here chiefly because
there was an opportunity to have a professional company. I have
refused to leave here for salaries much better than I get now because
I feel that professionalization is the answer to the whole situation
of theatre throughout the United States, and that it is somebody's
duty and privilege to preserve the professional type of theatre in
the country.

GARD: Just how does your type of professional Community
Theatre work? Where do you get the actors?

TARRANT: Well, in the first place, we have to get our actors from
sources that are compatible with our pay and also with our standards.
We have found that most of the people who have gone to New York
and suffered the disillusionments there for any length of time are
really and truly unsuited to a vital theatre life. They have lived
under some sort of reflected glory of sitting on the same stool at
Walgreen's that some famous star sat on when he or she was starv-
ing. And they have been under the influence of the illusion that they
are artists only if they wear their hair long and if they do strange
things.

Well, Erie is a Community Theatre in which our people must live
with the people of the community, and in which they have to work
hard. It's a glorious sweatshop. So where do we go for actors?
We go to the better schools of the country; to their graduates. We

find that many of the schools have many graduates who are no more ready to earn a living in theatre than they are to take political office in the national scene. But we find that occasionally there is an unusual talent fresh out of college who is capable of that. We find that, after a few seasons of summer stock, others are capable of living up to our standards, and so we bring people in on a trial basis, on fellowships. Our company is almost entirely built up from people who have been here on an eight-week fellowship and have tried out with us, or who have come on a full year-around apprenticeship.

GARD: How many people do you employ in your company?

TARRANT: Our company is probably at the lowest total level now that it has been since I have been at the Playhouse. We have just been emerging from a tough situation here in Erie. We have now on the staff six actors and four actresses, and backstage our staff is usually composed of a technical director and two assistants. Right now we have only one assistant backstage.

GARD: Do you supplement this paid company with volunteer or voluntary talent?

TARRANT: I think it is very important that the superior talent in the community be melded with the professional talent, and we do it every time we have a chance. There are a few people of real ability in the community, and from our student theatre we draw talent that is from a young level—the real young juvenile level. These people are trained in our schools and they are superior to many that we could hire to play in that young age range, so we use people in the community, especially, in large-cast shows extensively.

But I don't think we've touched on the real essence of professionalization. The professionalization of the Community Theatre involves risks, too. It involves problems of community relations that I think anyone who is contemplating professionalization should face. I don't mean that this should discourage them. It's like when you build a house . . . if your foundation is in quicksand, you put your piling in and you prepare for it. It doesn't stop you from building a house. When a theatre professionalizes, immediately there is a danger of siphoning off some of the community interest at the very devoted level because some of the sense of ownership is sacrificed. The average Community Theatre in the United States has largely been organized by people who wanted to act, who wanted to participate. When you lessen their opportunity to act, then you lose them.

And so I think it is very important in any professional theatre, especially at the smaller level, that there be definite provision made for extensive use of superior local talent and of letting it be an honor to develop in the craft to a professional level.

There is also a problem of scheduling professional theatre. To run without an extremely large endowment, or something of the sort, we must play every night, or at least six nights a week, to survive. This means that the people playing in the show are getting ready for a new show in the same way that summer stock prepares during the day. Your local participants who work in the daytime have the problem of scheduling to face. And we have found our greatest problem in using local talent is one of scheduling. Frequently, we will give our professional actors a little time off in the middle of the day and work them to the very last minute, just time enough so they can go and have dinner and get back for make-up, in order to rehearse a very talented volunteer young man or young lady who works until four-thirty or five in the afternoon.

GARD: The amateur learns from the professional, too.

TARRANT: Well, you know, the interesting thing is . . . if it's handled properly, the professional absorbs from the amateur, too. He gets an almost fanatical enthusiasm from the better volunteers, and you slough off the other ones very quickly. The interested and talented amateur absorbs from the professional a devotion of a more mature and, let's say, more enduring type of playing, because a professional must keep his level of interest going at a certain level throughout a year. He can't just say, "Goody, goody, we put on a show, and when the show is over we all have a big party and forget it for several weeks."

This weekend we are changing bills, and we will strike on Saturday night and go into dress rehearsal on Sunday afternoon. We rehearse again Sunday night and rehearse and work Monday, and we will have a performance for an invited audience on Monday night. We will open on Tuesday. With this type of intensive scheduling, something is bound to rub off on the amateurs to give them a mature approach.

GARD: I suppose that in your opinion the whole level of production has raised through this professional approach, and the standards of theatre in this community are also raised.

TARRANT: Definitely. There are several amateur groups operating here. We help them every way we can, and I think even their standards are somewhat raised by the fact of the presence of a professional group. Now, I don't want to be misunderstood on this. I have a tremendous respect for good amateurs. After all, the professional who is available to a low-budget company is not always as high in mentality or talent as maybe the young man who shows great promise but obeyed his father and became a lawyer, or a professor, or a doctor, or a successful businessman. So, frequently, there are occurrences of near genius, superior talent in amateurs, superior to anything that you can hire from the average run-of-the-mill professional sources. And so one feeds the other. As I say, there is an inspiration that comes from working with amateurs that is good for the professional, too, because the amateur is a one-shot actor and he will have several weeks to rest up and come up with vigor and vitality and maybe sometimes fumbling and stumbling.

GARD: How long has the Erie Playhouse been a professional house?

TARRANT: Well, it went professional, as I told you, when the thing changed over from very much a club operation. The first thing they saw, these men who took over, was that the standards must be raised, and so one professional actor was brought in and gradually others.

GARD: What year was that?

TARRANT: That was in the early thirties. I'm not sure exactly, but I would say that Erie had a professional staff by 1936 or so.

GARD: How about new plays and new playwrights? I know you are very much interested in that subject. What have you done here in Erie to support them?

TARRANT: Well, my conviction, of course, is that any theatre that has an excuse for survival plans its course in what it does for the movement as a whole. And I think the greatest crying need in the theatre is for writers. Actors by the thousands burn off because there is no place for them. Writers are needed. Broadway is hungry for writers, and now television is gobbling up writers with the appetite of some sort of a dragon; and so I think the greatest service Community Theatre can do is to develop new writers.

GARD: Do you often produce an original play?

TARRANT: Just as often as we can find one that we think is good enough to merit production and that we think has a chance to not cause us to lose too much money.

GARD: And how does the public accept original plays here?

TARRANT: They accept them. We get a few people excited about something new, but so far in insufficient numbers to pay the bills. We have to promote the play on some basis other than the fact that it's a new play.

Conversation with Frederic McConnell

Cleveland Play House, Cleveland, Ohio

Population—914,808

Frederic McConnell is small, white-haired, full of wisdom. As the Dean of American Community Theatre Directors, he has befriended many theatre aspirants both as Director of the Play House and as fellowships officer of the National Theatre Conference. Mr. McConnell believes that the core of any theatre is the ensemble —that the inner quality of a work is measured by the quality of the relations which unite its elements and assure continuity. He is a Scot, proud and dynamic. He studied under Thomas Wood Stevens at Carnegie Tech and received early spiritual help from Sam Hume of the Arts and Crafts Theatre in Detroit, and the Greek Theatre, University of California. He came to Cleveland in 1921, and under his leadership the Play House has become the foremost American professional Community Theatre. During the course of his conversation, one senses the depth of his experience.

The excellent Cleveland Play House plant, in land, buildings, and equipment, is worth about a million dollars. It consists of two buildings: the first was financed by three hundred individuals and a $100,000 loan from the bank, plus an outright gift of $50,000 worth of land upon which to build. There are two auditoriums: one seating 522, which is called Drury Theatre in honor of the donor of the site, and the Charles S. Brooks Theatre, seating 164. Built in 1927, the mortgage was paid off in ten years. The Euclid 77th Theatre was converted from a church to a new-old type of

CONVERSATION WITH FREDERIC McCONNELL   83

theatre, consisting of open forward apron, no curtain or proscenium, and a high-banked tier of seats in an arc around this stage. The value is around $350,000, and was financed through gifts and a bank loan, the latter being now substantially paid off.

The Play House is open to the public during an eight-month season of playing; about 150,000 seats are sold to defray the operating expenses of the shops, library, dressing rooms, technical offices, and social rooms, plus the salaries for more than sixty professional actors, directors, technicians, designers, and executive personnel. The staff contains mature and younger members. It associates amateurs, who through long association with the Play House have earned the right to the dignity of professionalism, includes guest artists and apprentice students who do resident work.

The repertory of the Play House includes from fourteen to twenty plays, depending upon the audience demand for extended runs. There is balance and variety in the choice, and both familiar and unknown works are produced. This institution does all it can to induce talented persons to write for the theatre.

Mr. McConnell has been at the forefront of the idea of a freer theatre, a professional theatre, so important to the Community Theatre idea. It is significant that the Ford Foundation has recently made an award of fifteen fellowships for talented, young professional actors to train at the Play House for three years. He has ideas about this, and about subsidy to American Theatre.

GARD: We've been talking about this problem of how to aid American theatre through subsidy. You were beginning to say something about a possible fellowship program. Do you want to enlarge on that idea?

McCONNELL: Yes. Now it's all part of the theory that has long since been accepted by most people—even people in New York—that the only way to save the American theatre is to make it possible for it to function nation-wide. It's generally agreed that the commercial theatre in New York can't possibly cover the territory in this great country—the way the whole theatre is set up there, it can't spread about. Various cities have done what they could to support "mushroom" community groups, some small and some large, and the net result has been that, strictly within the last twenty-five years, there is more of a public for the theatre in the isolated sections of the country than there was a generation ago.

I don't see any way to accomplish a creating of interest in the theatre except by making it possible for the theatre to exist in centers throughout the nation. There's a catch to it as it now stands, and that is that, as stated in an article in the *New York Times* a couple of weeks ago, as far as New York is concerned, and New York is reflected elsewhere, the theatre now is dependent upon a hit-happy public. The theatre cannot survive that way, because, in the first place, there are not enough hit shows written.

If we rely on hits only we are going to starve. This leads up to the essential importance of an established institutional theatre in the various communities that can operate over a season of eight or nine months. While they may occasionally do one of these hit plays, they can also produce other plays that are of importance—comedies as well as serious drama.

But for those regional Community Theatres to function they must have personnel, and while many of them can support their own personnel, yet any aid that they could receive from either local foundations or national foundations in the way of fellowships makes them work that much better.

Now the other angle of the fellowship situation is that the universities, and there are many fine ones (their theatre departments are turning out well-trained graduates in the theatre in various branches of acting, technical work, designing, and playwriting; but they have no place to go, as has been said many times too, and it's very true), through a far-flung fellowship program would provide placement over two or three years for these promising graduates where they could earn a living or support themselves in practicing a craft which they have very painfully, over four years, been learning to develop.

As it is now, some go into teaching and some just get discouraged, and don't go into theatre at all. This is surely a great loss.

GARD: Now, how about dreaming a little bit? You speak of a far-flung fellowship program. How would you ideally like to see such a fellowship program work, and from where would it operate?

McCONNELL: Well, let's speak in terms of figures. Say an appropriation of a million dollars was made by a foundation, or a group of foundations, to distribute after careful selection, careful study, a great number of fellowships around the country in important centers. Here the fellow not only would be surrounded by people with greater experience than himself, professionally speaking (so that he could advance in his work because of being surrounded by people who have been at it longer), but he, in turn, because of his training in a college or in a Community Theatre, would be a great asset to the center itself. In other words, a reciprocal arrangement.

Now I would say flatly that I think the fellowship plan should be administered by some officer, or some office, in the foundation that contributes the money. In the first place, the foundation has great financial resources as well as prestige. It can go into a community and investigate the center to determine whether that institution (the Cleveland Play House, for example) is worthy of a fellowship, and whether the fellow can gain in creativity in that theatre. You need some guarantee that foundation money wasn't being wasted, and self-administration of a program by a foundation would be one way to assure that.

GARD: In other words, the chief problem would be to discover some way to find out who likely candidates were, how they could be referred to a central fellowship agency.

McCONNELL: It could be done two ways. One, the institution itself would make application, even to the extent of nominating by name, description, photograph, history, background, education, two or three people whom they would guarantee, or would like to absorb in the organization. The other way would be a combination. There would be a field man who would go around and meet institutions on the ground and make his own evaluation of their integrity and of the value to the community, and he would recommend back to the central office, "Yes, I've been through this institution. I have seen what they do, I have learned something about their influence in the community, met some of their trustees, talked to the dramatic critics in that community, even stopped to the point of seeing a play—" Sometimes these traveling interviewers don't stay to see a play, and they don't really get their hand on the pulse of the institution. However, a field representative's recommendation or endorsement of the application, I think, would be somewhat essential.

GARD: In your opinion, would Community Theatres, and now

I'm speaking of the ones that have been longest established and have proved by their very existence of twenty or more years that they are an integral part of community cultural life—in your opinion, what would be the response of such Community Theatres to this kind of fellowship program?

McCONNELL: That's a very delicate question. It's an ironic fact that in many cases the Community Theatre will say we don't want subsidy help. They might be glad to have help in building a building or pay off a mortgage, but they might like to preserve the volunteer integrity of the organization.

Now there are some—I know one theatre anyway, don't mind mentioning what it is, it's the Tulsa Little Theatre directed by Theodore Viehman—which has crossed that bridge, and he knows, and I know too, from experience, that you still can maintain the validity and the spirit of your volunteer organization, and have at your beck and call a few assistants whom you need if you are going to produce well: and the whole function of all these local theatres is *to produce well.*

In most cases the only theatre that exists is community. So you can blend with your volunteer organization a few people who are more experienced, and who are devoting their lives to the art of the theatre. Of course it takes tactful handling.

GARD: Would you say, then, that a certain kind of professionalism or professionalization, not complete, but a certain amount of it, is apt to increase the receptivity of the Community Theatre in the community itself, as well as raising a total set of standard values?

McCONNELL: I'm sure of that. I know it's been a question many years within the confines of the National Theatre Conference, and elsewhere, that it can't be done; but I think the trouble is that people, seeing the difficulties, think of professionalizing all at once —throwing out their whole volunteer organization and bringing in a new so-called "professional nucleus." But if they do it slowly and do it by integrating members of the community who have been active with this theatre over the years, they are still keeping a large part of the same personnel.

I know that a few assistants, if they handle themselves correctly and are really competent people, will earn the respect of the people in the theatre who are on a volunteer basis and will be helpful to them.

GARD: As I understand it, the major point you are making is that a foundation, or series of foundations, could make their major impact on American theatre, or, I'd rather say, theatre in American community life, through support of a certain kind of professionalization through fellowships to outstanding people, who might function as professional assistants along with the volunteers or voluntary group in the community. Am I stating it correctly?

McCONNELL: Yes, you are. Except we've got to find another word to take the place of professionalization, because professionalization implies in many people's minds that somehow it is connected to the commercial theatre, and the real professional is something more than just a commercial worker.

GARD: You mean . . . something like an aesthetic professionalism. Or a professional point of view without necessarily a commercial necessity attached to it. In selecting these people, this professional corps of workers, what branches of theatre art would you go after first? Would you go after playwrights, and try to get them rooted in the community? This is something that some playwrights seem to want—attachment to a theatre. For instance, in the smaller communities, is there any place for a professional playwright connected with a Community Theatre group?

McCONNELL: There's a place for him, but the first approach, I think, should be in the acting-directing field. Most of our Community Theatres, our good ones, are blessed with well-trained and good directors. That is not where we are lacking. What is needed everywhere is good actors.

GARD: I agree with you in part. The top level is well off for directors. The smaller groups are not.

McCONNELL: The playwright might spend two years with a group and write a play, but the community would not be the beneficiary of that creation maybe for several years—just in terms of one month's playing of his script. But with the actor or the director or the designer, it's the case of a man or woman functioning in a creative and expressive, articulate way, helping to improve the work that that theatre does.

I might be old-fashioned in this, but I certainly have plenty of

support for the theory from dramatic critics and from a lot of playwrights that the best way, perhaps the *only* way, to write a play
is to have an idea and to go off somewhere and write it. Essentially
a play's a written document, and I think it should be done mostly
in the privacy of the writer's room and his own soul—with an
amount of practical theatre experience attached, of course.

GARD: The playwright, with you then, would not be the primary
problem, but rather the expressive artist seems in your estimation
to be the important thing to go after? You would want to get hold
of people with outstanding creative points of view, boldness, fear-
less approaches? In other words, I'm trying to get you to characterize the type of person that you would think ideal for fellowship or
staff assignment.

McCONNELL: I think the same rule that you would apply to this
ideal person you would apply to his activity in other aspects of life.
In other words, a young lawyer or young doctor or young teacher
to be successful and useful to our society—the more imagination
he has the better, the more straight thinking he does the better.
Health, of course, is important; and on the stage, naturally, personality counts a great deal—maybe too much. Audiences clamor for
that. If you don't like the word personality, call it personal mag-
netism—something within him that creates an empathy between
him and the audience.

Now that isn't quite so vital with a bank president, lawyer, or
doctor. So, as far as the theatre is concerned, the people who come
out of the schools, those who have a creative, expressive talent, are
the most valuable. They are more valuable than those who have
only a book knowledge of the theatre, only a literary concept of it.
Because they have to get out there in front of the audience and
create something.

GARD: What would you think of the general idea of having some
kind of a selection board, drawn from outstanding Community
Theatres in America, be the final judges both of the candidates who
might be proposed for this sort of fellowship program and also the
board would select the places where such candidates might go?
Would that have any value?

McCONNELL: I think that's clumsy. I believe the other I proposed a moment ago is quickest, easiest, and cheapest. Say you have

a board of six or seven people in this part of the country. All right! There's the expense of getting them together at a central meeting place. Then there's the added expense of all these candidates coming to them, and presumably the local institution or the foundation itself would have to pay for that. Well—you have sat on enough boards to know—what can you learn about people in maybe a couple of days? Especially about their creative abilities?

GARD: I agree with you, and I guess what I am thinking of was more the placement of such people, because I would think that one of the objectives of this kind of program might be to get some of these creative folk in places or situations that needed bucking up. Whether the individual himself would have such a place in mind, I don't know. I doubt it. And one of the things that worries me a little bit is the set of prestige values that has been built up. New York City, as a place in itself, has a prestige value for the ordinary person who wants to go ahead in the theatre arts. There must be a lot of American spots that are doing good creative work that are not known, that have no prestige value whatever, and yet with the added aid of a fellowship program might actually amount to more and have a wider sphere of influence.

McCONNELL: You mean, if a fellow were sent to a small community by a reputable foundation or some nationally known organization, it would give prestige within the citizens of that community?

GARD: It might give some prestige, and I think might actually help break down the spotty idea that we have in America that certain places have prestige and other places do not, which perhaps is a disease of our contemporary society.

McCONNELL: It's very true. I'm sure that in a small community a good person who came there with the blessing or nomination from a disinterested organization like a foundation, would mean more to that community in terms of prestige than if somebody gave a director five thousand dollars to go to Broadway and hire an actress. The latter thing is snobbish, the other way is solid and also the candidate is likely to be somebody who doesn't come from the so-called "rat race" in the Big City. It was a long time ago, but this book that Norris Houghton wrote under a Rockefeller Grant—well, Norris says somewhere in the book * that this country is teeming

* *Advance From Broadway,* by Norris Houghton.

with young people who have tremendous potential theatre possibilities. And the tragedy is that those people aren't being tapped before they lose interest or go into other activities. So there's a mine of material there. Gradually some of them get to New York, struggle around, and make a place for themselves. But New York, as the professional theatre center, does not need to make it the source of our material. It's much better to go to the University of Wisconsin and spend a day talking with you, or Arnold Gillette out at the University of Iowa, or John Reich at Goodman, or Canfield at Yale, or talk with Barclay Leathem at Western Reserve.

GARD: In summing it up, would you say that the kind of program you have described could do more to further American theatre in American places than anything that you could think of right off the bat?

MCCONNELL: I don't think offhand that there could be a more progressive, a more creative, a more natural help than some such fellowship program.

GARD: And the major idea, as far as getting the American people to be receptive to theatre, would be, in your opinion, the creation of better production, of better plays produced superbly well by competent people.

MCCONNELL: It's the same theory that a symphony orchestra is more likely to appeal to the larger public, because they are experienced players, than any sort of a community orchestra. A community orchestra does a lot of good, especially to the people of the orchestra, but I don't know that it has great impact unless it can play great music in a great manner.

GARD: In other words, the hard core of theatre in the community is the well-produced play itself?

MCCONNELL: Well, that's the maximum. And the minimum would have value, also. The minimum would be to produce theatre, period. The better it is, fine; but the only way to get people interested in the theatre is to get them in it.

GARD: Now, I have one more question I want to ask you. This, too, is a knotty one. We are not building many playhouses in America right now. How important do you think architecture is to the development of a new concept, or a growing concept, of

American theatre? If we had better playhouses or better places to play, would that make any material difference?

McCONNELL: Now, by better, do you mean in aesthetic architectural design, or do you mean in function?

GARD: I mean in both. I was in Chicago, for instance, and was taken all around these combination fieldhouses where the theatre groups of the Chicago Park District play. There are fifteen community groups in the District and they said that their major problem was the lack of proper facilities—that was what I heard over and over again in Chicago. How important do you think a playhouse, as a thing in and of itself, is, as being a symbol in the community of theatre arts?

McCONNELL: Well, this may not be a direct answer. How well do you think a painter would get along if he had neither a canvas nor paint, nor perhaps a brush? One thing I think we have to avoid in our whole attitude toward the theatre, toward staging, is that we don't subscribe too much or too arbitrarily to the conventions of what I choose to call the old theatre.

The old theatre goes from, well, about early nineties through the twenties or the thirties—a very small section of our theatrical history in terms of several thousand years.

Now we shouldn't be a slave to our equipment, except our basic equipment, such as good lighting systems, for nowadays, as you know, a light accomplishes more than anything else really. On the other hand, we shouldn't be overloaded with wagons and cycloramas, and mechanical gadgets to which we become slaves. That's one reason I wanted to show you our Euclid Avenue Theatre, it's a complete departure from the conventional theatre of this country. It's entirely open; there is no proscenium as such, a big apron goes out in front. It's patterned after the Elizabethan stage and the Graeco-Roman theatre. But we are not a slave to doing only Shakespeare or Greek tragedies, because we have proved in the last seven or eight years that you can do a so-called "realistic" play as effectively in our Euclid Theatre as anywhere else, in fact more so, because the audience is in close contact with the actor and the play.

GARD: You know, you sound more and more like our Wisconsin architect, Frank Lloyd Wright. He was hitting it awfully hard

that a democracy needs things in and of itself, and that we have
no direct need to copy from anybody.

McCONNELL: Well, that's right. I was invited to make a speech
at the Southwest Theatre Conference in Dallas a year ago, and they
were starting to build a theatre that Mr. Wright was engaged to do.
We were among friends there, and I made some remark—you
know, you have to make some kind of wisecrack in the course of a
speech—that Mr. Wright for many years had been in the blueprint
stage in regard to this new type of noncommercial theatre, but that
in the meantime, in 1949, the Cleveland Play House built the darn
thing and Mr. Wright's plans are still on the drawing board.

One reason for that is that his ideas were frightfully extravagant
and he's inclined to try to combine too many mechanical gadgets
that really are now obsolete with the theory of the open space.

A great problem in the theatre in this country, not only for the
Community Theatre, but for the Broadway theatre and the amateur
theatre, is the paucity of the plays. Now, I don't know what the
answer to that is, whether playwrights are decreasing, or going
elsewhere, or spending too much time in Hollywood, or not writing
for the theatre because the reward in the theatre is not, financially
anyway, as great as it used to be.

Probably one of the incentives for a playwright would be the
knowledge that we are beginning to build independent theatre organizations throughout the country which to some extent might make
up for the disappearance of the old-fashioned road theatre which
offered some market. In other words, the market will become a little
bigger. Not enough to become really lucrative, but certainly lucrative enough to justify a playwright sticking to his last. This goes
back to what I said earlier, that the theatre cannot survive in New
York or any place else merely on the occasional, sensational hit
play. All we know in New York now, in professional theatre, is that
it's either a smash or it's a failure. There is no room commercially
for the so-called "middle-ground" play that a respectable audience
still exists for today. The audiences don't get a chance to see it.

These theatres around the country, whether they are professional
or amateur, are able to do many of these so-called "middle-ground"
plays with success; and the reason they can do that is, first, because
they do operate on a season basis and, second, their cost of opera-

tion is much lower than if they were strictly commercial theatre. The gamble isn't as great.

It seems right now that the theatre in America has to be subsidized in some way. Somebody pointed out to me the other day that the New York theatre is just as much subsidized as a theatre in a local community that receives a grant from somebody. Though they don't call it subsidy in New York, it *is* subsidy. It just means that some Wall Street gambler is subsidizing that production, hoping to make some money or to relieve his tax situation. Some don't really care whether they lose the money or not.

GARD: What about this movement of the revival of classics here and there over the country, which has had quite a little bit of popularity? Should such classical-revival theatres be subsidized?

McCONNELL: You mean places like Stratford, Ontario, or Connecticut? Well, certainly, there is a kind of sentiment about them because of Mr. Shakespeare. They should be helped, providing help doesn't stop there.

GARD: In other words, it shouldn't be a thing in and of itself, but rather only one pebble on a whole beach of pebbles.

McCONNELL: Take Stratford, the Canadian Stratford. It received a tremendous sum of money sometime ago. I think it was from the Rockefeller Foundation. They couldn't have operated without that money, and yet that's just one pebble. They're spreading it around in Canada, because they have organized a traveling company that goes around and gives a presentation of their summer plays.

GARD: Personally, you would place that kind of subsidy on a lower level or at a lower priority than your fellowship program idea?

McCONNELL: I don't know. I wouldn't want to evaluate that too strictly because you can argue both ways. I'm sure that the fellowship program has a greater spread and would help the country more as a whole; but a fine Shakespearean season at Stratford, Ontario, and the one at Connecticut, does a great deal of good for the thousands of people who come from afar to see it. There's one thing about these Shakespeare Festivals; so far, I think they are all summer activities.

GARD: The summertime theatre probably ought to be a special area of consideration, perhaps.

McCONNELL: Yes, so far as the classics—Shakespeare—is concerned. But the average summer theatre, which is purely a private commercial venture, might be permitted to struggle by itself. Speaking of Shakespeare, of course there is a lot of Shakespearean work going on 'n the country that the country doesn't know about. At the Play House here, for fifteen years, we have had what we call a Shakespeare Festival, which is a series of special weekday matinees for high-school students in this area. In fact, they are growing so that people are coming now from all parts of the state. We've done about twelve plays, mostly comedies; but the point is, it goes along for about a month and it brings students from all schools in this area to the theatre. Certainly with most of them it's the first time they have ever seen a Shakespeare.

Our Shakespeare Festival isn't dominated by stars, it's just our own company; but they are good enough to induce the Board of Education of Cleveland to support us and excuse the boys and girls for an afternoon. One local critic here rather cynically said, "Well, sure, your Shakespearean Festival is successful; it's a good way of getting out of class for a couple of hours." But I think it serves a greater purpose than that. It plays to about 11,000 students.

GARD: What new techniques do you employ to interest the average citizen, the chap who might spend his evening in a tavern, to get him into the living theatre?

McCONNELL: I can tell you one that we have adopted here and at Pittsburgh. That is to spend considerable energy and money on what we call "group sales." In other words, we go to the factories in this community (and there are a great many), to the public-relations director, and we provide an evening at the Play House for a group of twenty-five to five hundred at a very special price. The public-relations man very wisely does not press this because he is also afraid of fraternalism. He offers the opportunity for the people in the factory, especially the white-collar workers, to come as a group at a reduced price, and after the show they will have a little *kaffeeklatsch* with the actors in a social way. I'm sure a lot of those people, if left alone, wouldn't come. We have learned that many of these individuals have come back later, bringing their wives or friends, and some have become subscribers to the season. That's a slow process, but it's tapping an audience that never would come on its own.

GARD: I believe that American industry is coming closer than it ever has been to an awareness of the theatre arts. They use theatre a lot in their training programs, many of the industries do. Some of them even employ their own drama directors, not just as recreation necessarily, although that may be a part of it, but as actual portrayal of different techniques in salesmanship, or helping to put across a major idea. It's theatre on a pretty low level but it is, I think, an awareness at least of dramatic technique.

McCONNELL: It's a type of schooling for these men that is not just lectures.

GARD: That's exactly right.

McCONNELL: I saw something—well, I see it every night as a matter of fact. The Gulf Oil Company has a traveling unit which goes from one station to another instructing by demonstration how employees should handle the gas pump, what they should say to a customer and not say, which makes it a bit more interesting. They make it more interesting for those prospective employees— not just a handbook or a talk.

Conversation with Kendrick Wilson

Omaha Community Playhouse
Omaha, Nebraska
Population—251,117

Kendrick Wilson is a brilliant director and a fine actor. His loyalties to Omaha go very deep, and he has led a campaign which has built a beautiful new theatre for this most typical of Middle West cities. Citizens of Omaha are inclined to believe that good theatre originates in Omaha; they don't need to travel elsewhere to see fine plays.

In conversation Wilson speaks quickly, makes points sharply. He is slender and tall, full of tough strength.

GARD: This is your thirteenth season with the Omaha Playhouse?

WILSON: Yes, except for two and a half years in the army. I came here first in 1942.

GARD: And the population of Omaha is about 300,000?

WILSON: Right.

GARD: Does the Board of Trustees interfere with you to any noticeable extent as far as administration or operation? Is the Board developed as a working committee?

WILSON: Yes. We try to keep about half the Board people who are interested in theatre problems gained from helping with acting, or production, or people who have a theatre knowledge. The other half of the Board is composed of civic-minded individuals who merely want to attend the theatre. They are very valuable in fund-raising and publicity, and they give us a more accurate public opinion as to what people want in Omaha theatre.

96

GARD: What about play selection? Does the Board leave that up to you?

WILSON: No, play selection is handled by a play-reading committee. Usually, I recommend plays to a play-reading committee, and some of them will come up with their own ideas. I recommend about twice the number of shows we might do. The Board has the final say-so. They have to approve the selections, and in the thirteen years I've only done one show that I didn't want to do. That was a horse trade, a swap for a show I did want to do, so I can't complain. There have been shows I would like to do, but haven't done. In the end the Board has usually proved themselves right.

GARD: Is the Playhouse in debt or has it ever been in debt?

WILSON: They were in debt when I first came here in 1942. And, of course, they had a mortgage on this building which they hadn't paid off. They were a couple of thousand dollars in debt then; right now we are well in the black.

GARD: The community in general supports the Playhouse then. Could you characterize for me Omaha as a place in which to operate a playhouse? Would you say Omaha's a particularly good theatre community? Is it unique in any way?

WILSON: It's *very* typically Middle Western, and it is so typical that it is unique.

GARD: Now would you go on with that a little?

WILSON: The greatest advantage in operating the Playhouse is that there's so little other activity . . . so little competition other than a fine symphony, which people who like music attend. Some of them come to see us, too. Of a more recognizable nature, we have no competition in natural entertainment. That is, we have no lakes; people don't fish or boat on the Missouri River. There's nothing else to do in town. You can go bowling, drinking, golfing, or go to the Playhouse, and there's practically no other theatre activity. About once in two years we get a road company, a legitimate play, and the alternate year we get a musical.

GARD: What about the public taste?

WILSON: The public taste is a normal, average American taste.

GARD: In your operation do you have any set purpose or reason for operating? For instance, John Young at Shreveport claims their main purpose is to operate a family theatre in the sense of family entertainment. Now do you have any such point of view?

WILSON: No. Family entertainment gets very difficult, and so frequently your margin on the sophistication side is whether the whole family should come or want to come. Some do and some don't. Actually, as far as the family theatre is concerned, it's impractical on the finance side. People who have two or three kids . . . very few of them can afford to come. And they certainly can't bring families on Friday or Saturday night, when the children might come, because there's no room. So we try to give as much variety in a season as possible. We try to please at least everyone once during the season and not disappoint them more than once.

GARD: What has been your current season's bill?

WILSON: *Time Limit, Chalk Garden, Desperate Hours* . . . can't remember our second show at the moment.

GARD: In other words, you give a variety of kinds of plays— comedy and serious. Do you try a classic every once in a while?

WILSON: Every once in a while, yes; not too often. Those who like classics like them very, very, much; but there are too many people who stay away. And those who do come . . . well, about half of them will really like it and half of them won't.

GARD: You don't have any particular plan, then, of exposing the community to classical stuff?

WILSON: Not on a definite plan. We do keep raising their taste little by little, year by year, by every once in a while filling in with a classic or semi-classic. But we seldom tell them they are seeing a classic.

GARD: Do you think the same people come back production after production, or does your audience change?

WILSON: It's pretty much the same people inasmuch as our membership of over three thousand takes care of 80 per cent of our capacity on a fourteen-night run. Now as far as membership turnover is concerned, there's about a 20 per cent fall-off each year of people who leave town, get sick or too old, get mad at us for a particular play, or decide to spend their money some place else next year. Some people will buy a Playhouse membership one year and Symphony membership the next. I think they are smart, if they can't afford both.

GARD: What kind of staff do you have besides yourself?

WILSON: There is a full-time technical director. Then there's a part-time technical assistant who comes in a couple of hours a day to clean up, wash buckets, sweep . . . amounts to a backstage janitor. Then we have a part-time janitor taking care of the rest of the building and the yard, and a part-time box-office attendant. That's it.

GARD: The rest of the assistance is entirely volunteer. You pay no actors . . . nothing of that sort. What is your point of view on the payment of actors, in a Community Theatre, that is? If you had the funds to do it, do you think it would be a good idea?

WILSON: *If* we had the funds to do it, I think it would be a good idea to pay the actors that we use inasmuch as it costs them a considerable amount in cash in order to give up six weeks, night after night that they do, for rehearsals and performances. I'm not enthused at all about a permanent paid acting staff or acting company. I think it would limit or restrict us in the quality of play that we aim at. I can indulge in type casting that I couldn't indulge in with a permanent staff of paid actors. We get better quality, I think, under our present operation. Even if we were paying the staff, I would still have open tryouts for casting, because the audience likes variety. They don't want to see all the same faces. They like to recognize some of them and see new faces they haven't seen before.

GARD: You think a professionalization of the Community Theatre ought to be in terms of presenting as professional a production as you can, but not characterizing professionalism purely in terms of monetary reimbursement?

WILSON: As far as paying, every once in a while I'm sorely tempted to pay one of the radio or TV actors who is on nights, so they could afford to come with us for one show. It would be good and healthy, but we don't. At the present time we can't afford it.

GARD: Professionalism, then, as far as your operation, is an *attitude* rather than a reality of money?

WILSON: Right.

GARD: What is your point of view on the presentation of original plays?

WILSON: If I could get the original scripts, I would like to do them. We've done two. I've been reading scripts, anywhere from ten to twenty scripts a year, and I don't find any that are worth the effort.

GARD: Have you made any attempts to encourage playwriting in Nebraska, or in this city?

WILSON: One of the plays that we did was by an Omaha author. It was a dramatization of a short story she had written. The other one we did was by a boy who formerly played at the Playhouse, worked here and then went on. I suppose that's encouragement to some extent, although nothing ever happened to either script. After they were done here, that was the end of it.

GARD: You would be willing to produce good, original work if it were available?

WILSON: Yes, if it were available.

GARD: What is your attitude toward having, if one were ever available to you, a playwright-in-residence attached to the Omaha Community Playhouse?

WILSON: That would depend on the individual.

GARD: In other words, in theory you would have nothing against its happening, providing the person was the right person?

WILSON: Providing he was the right person and had proper ideas about himself and his work—as to where it fits. Our public is not interested in new scripts as such. We would not draw an additional person by advertising that we were doing a world première. In fact, some people would stay away. What they want to see is those that have been heard about, which means the shows that have been popular in New York. That's what they want to pay their money for. They *will* come to an original script because we are doing it, and we can get away with it on the basis of the reputation of the other shows we do. We throw it in and some of our public like it, but most of them wouldn't, unless the show itself were of the best to compare with Broadway. That's what the original scripts are competing with, and that's hard. They are competing with scripts that have been tested, rewritten, proven, and have become successful.

GARD: Have you ever had in your membership here any major quarrel arising out of anything in the operation of the Playhouse?

WILSON: No split within the Board. There are bound to be con-

troversial issues coming up with plays that you do and they result
sometimes in community splits.

GARD: Have you had any clash between this leader and that
leader, or this strong personality or that, which led to a splitting up
of the group?

WILSON: No, not while I have been here that I heard of, nor
anything of importance before that.

GARD: In other words, you probably keep pretty close watch on
that sort of thing. You know how to deal with it.

WILSON: Well, our Board is again unique, I suppose, in that it
has no one strong, strong leader. It has no one person who is the
sponsor of the theatre. There are twenty-four individuals on the
Board, each with his own opinion, and they never line up on the
same side.

GARD: There are no cliques, then, within the Board or within the
membership that you know about?

WILSON: No. In other words, there is no member of the Board
that I have to bow to a little more than some of the others. I treat
them all alike.

GARD: Do you have any policy or system of training leaders
within the group itself?

WILSON: Policy or system, no. We do an awful lot of leadership
training, but it's indirect. We never know who's going to show up
for the first time on a prop crew or paint crew and then develop an
interest to become stage manager or an actor. You are usually surprised to see who hangs on year after year. Leadership just develops
naturally.

GARD: If you find a good actor or actress, do you tend to cast
him in several parts during the season?

WILSON: It happens sometimes. I don't intend to. . . . I try to
avoid it, if possible. I try to pass parts around as much as I can, but
I have to keep in mind on casting the major controlling policy for
the entire operation: that the Playhouse is operated for the membership, and membership is the audience; so that the emphasis in
casting must be what cast will give me the best results for this play.
If I have to use somebody I used in the last play, I do. If I don't
need to use them, I don't, so that really solves the problem. As far
as the girls are concerned, they are seldom in more than one show

a year, unless an actress is really unusual; and at that she'd have to be very versatile in order to play in two or three. Now Cherie Shaver, you met her a little while ago, has been playing in two a year the last two years. But out of four parts, none of them are alike; and she can do Cockney, which is rare. Some of the men have occasionally played in all six shows of the season, but never six leads. Some of those would be bit parts, and we don't have as many men coming out. As you know, there are more men's parts in practically every play. Most of the men who play leads are apt to play in only one show a year. That's all the time they can afford.

GARD: What do you think may be the most serious problem facing American Community Theatre?

WILSON: Direction. When a Community Theatre looks for a director now, it's a chore. To find an experienced one is almost impossible, particularly for the smaller theatres that don't have a large budget, and even the large theatres that do have the budget are hard put to find a man of considerable experience. They just are not available.

GARD: What do you think the qualifications of a Community Theatre director ought to be?

WILSON: First of all, he must be an individual who wants to do nothing but theatre. You must be married to theatre far beyond the money you might get out of it. Of course, there are a lot of people married to theatre, but you must have an interest in all sides of the theatre. A man can't confine himself to just directing or acting. He's got to know the technical end of the theatre even though he does have a technician-designer, and most Community Theatres don't have one. He's got to have a knowledge of public relations and publicity values. He has all of those volunteers to guide and channel, in addition to the ordinary production of the shows. He has to keep his fingers in all kinds and sides of the theatre. He may even have to do a little bookkeeping now and then.

GARD: How many people does your present theatre hold?

WILSON: Two hundred and fifty, and our new theatre will hold five hundred and fourteen.

GARD: Yes, I'd heard that you were building a new one. Do you think you will be able to fill your new house for most performances?

WILSON: Well, from the experience at Tulsa and Des Moines and

Denver and Indianapolis and the others that have built new theatres, or have improved their old theatres, they found that with the new comforts for the audience their membership doubled. I expect the same thing will happen here. We'll go from three thousand to six thousand within a couple of years.

GARD: From what kinds of sources did you raise the money for the new Playhouse?

WILSON: Oh, that's a question I like to answer, because that's a little unique here. We had a professional fund-raiser helping with it, and that is what I would advocate for anybody who wants to raise over $100,000. He had definitely said that, for our goal of $300,000, we had to have one gift of between $75,000 and $100,000. Well, that gift never did materialize. In fact, our largest single gift was $25,000. We had two of these, one from the clearinghouse of banks and the other from the newspaper. The next largest gift was $10,000 from an individual, and then it jumped down to $7,500. There were three or four of those. We had no backlog or backing from any one individual for any major portion of our drive. Most of the gifts came from firms and individuals varying from $500 to $1,000, and a much larger share than was normal in a campaign of this kind was from the general public in gifts of five dollars to fifty dollars, which keeps us truly a Community Theatre.

GARD: What is it costing you to build your new plant?

WILSON: Our preliminary estimates on costs run $500,000, which I think is a little high. Actually, as of March, 1959, the cost will be about $550,000, and we have cash in the bank in pledges at the present time for $330,000. That amount is the result of the fund-raising campaign we conducted a year ago at this time, plus $25,000 we made off our production of the show, The Country Girl, with Henry Fonda and Dorothy McGuire. Where the other $200,000 comes from is a little debatable at this point. We're going ahead and build the theatre and will leave off an office wing and the canopy at the front, which is the main part of the decor of the exterior of the building. We open in August and are in hopes that there will be an angel who'll come to our rescue or partial rescue once we get building, but we have got to keep faith with the people who have made donations. Besides, the Omaha Fire Department is going to kick us out of this building within a year anyway.

GARD: You mentioned Henry Fonda. Was he an Omaha boy?

WILSON: Yes, he started out right here on this stage. He was an actor, technician, and janitor here for the Playhouse. He got $500 a year building the scenery and taking care of all the cleaning, sidewalk shoveling, everything.

And, also Dorothy McGuire started here.

Conversation with Theodore Viehman

Tulsa Little Theatre
Tulsa, Oklahoma
Population—182,740

Ted Viehman, tall, quiet, dignified, and effective, is a philosopher of American Community Theatre. Greatly respected in the whole community of Tulsa, he has made the Tulsa group outstanding in the entire Southwest. His operation is one of the largest and most completely successful, especially in the number of persons he involves in every production. Yet his standards are very high. He is an artist first, a sociologist and recreationist second. He is nationally known, and has contributed vital ideas to the development of American regional theatre. In conversation he is sturdy, staying with an idea until all sides have been clarified. His wife, Gerda, is indispensable, gracious, ever helpful—a perfect mate for a Community Theatre director.

GARD: How long has the Tulsa Little Theatre been in existence?
VIEHMAN: We are in our thirty-seventh year with about two hundred major productions to our credit. Uninterrupted production since 1923. There have been no seasons when no production work was done.
GARD: Who was responsible for the founding of the theatre?
MRS. VIEHMAN: As a matter of fact, it was first started by a small group of women who were originally connected with the American Association of University Women. It started with Mrs. Holway and Mrs. Black and Bonnie Reed, and it grew from that.

105

VIEHMAN: One of the unique things about the Tulsa Little Theatre is that it only went two years without a paid trained director; so that the past thirty-three years it has always had a full-time (at least one) paid man to direct their activities.

GARD: How long has the Tulsa Little Theatre had its own theatre?

MRS. VIEHMAN: This building was first started in 1929. Before that it was in a rented place.

VIEHMAN: However, the theatre as it stands today is quite different from what it was in 1929, because out of surpluses from year to year we have made additions to the theatre. At the present time the plant consists of about six additions to what was the original theatre, and there has never been any subsidy whatever. Everything that has been done has been done out of surpluses. I'm not sure that that is the best thing that could happen, but it's been the American style of growth.

Actually, today we have a membership of about 7,500 and we play to about that many people, not all members, for we also have a box-office sale. Our growth has been from about 1,800 members fifteen years ago. The budget, fifteen years ago, totaled about $8,500 at the box office. Now we operate on about a budget of $65,000, playing approximately three weeks of every play and doing six a year. At the present time, of course, there are two production people, a director and an assistant director, and two box-office people full-time.

GARD: I'd like to ask you about the kind of people who come to the Tulsa Little Theatre productions. Do they represent a cross-section of the population of the city? It's not a prestige activity or a club activity?

MRS. VIEHMAN: No, it's not a club activity. Our members come from all walks of life.

VIEHMAN: I would say it's a cross-section of the discriminating people of the city. After all, everybody in our big city is not interested in theatre, but more and more of them are coming to get entertainment.

MRS. VIEHMAN: This town—the background of this town—is a little different from some. It has a high percentage of, shall we say, middle-class people. We receive a good share of our patronage from people who are clerks in the oil companies, for example. Of course, it's a very wealthy town, too. The general type of people is a different type from that you will find in some cities.

GARD: What do you charge for tickets?

VIEHMAN: The membership is $7.50 a year, which admits the holder to one performance of each of the six plays. You can't use those six tickets indiscriminately. If they don't go to the third play, they lose that. Then, if they are not members and want to pay at the box office, they pay $2.00 straight, so that the advantage in being a member is obvious.

GARD: One of the things that I am very much interested in is the matter of standards or levels of appreciation in the community. Have you ever had outstanding success with classic drama in Tulsa?

VIEHMAN: Yes. In fact, the plays that are best remembered, although not necessarily at the time the biggest attendance, are plays like *A Midsummer Night's Dream, Twelfth Night, Skin of Our Teeth, The Crucible.* Everybody who came found that they had a tremendously good time seeing that play.

Of course, if you were playing in Community Theatre in a large city to 25,000 people, the average taste level is higher than if you are playing to 7,500 people. And the way that we have answered that is to vary our program. In six plays we have sort of a pattern. About half the plays will be Broadway comedy successes; but we always reserve at least one, and usually two, spots for the quality plays. We feel that's necessary, because unless we do the quality plays we do not satisfy that hard core—they are a minority— people who have been with us for fifteen to twenty-five years, and always come and look for those better plays. If they don't get them, we are going to lose friends; and our discerning friends are the mainstay of the theatre, not the casual attendant who comes for entertainment alone. So in order to pay our bills we take a middle ground, keep our feet on the ground, and do the so-called "popular" plays; but we always insist, year after year, on doing quality plays to satisfy that more discriminating part of our audience, even though they are a minority.

MRS. VIEHMAN: Once a year we do one big effort, and *Tiger at the Gates,* which we have just closed, has been our big effort for this year.

GARD: Would you care to make any judgment as to how this kind of middle-ground program has affected the success of the Tulsa Little Theatre? Has it been able to exist longer and more successfully because of this middle ground?

VIEHMAN: Probably, although there are other factors that enter into the Tulsa Little Theatre's success. First of all, we have always put emphasis on high standards of work. We feel very bad when we have a bad show. The net result has been that quality in our theatre is such that we have very little competition. I mean competition from other civic groups.

Many cities and Community Theatre people suffer from the fact that they have four or five competitive groups, none of them able to command all the resources of the city. The result is that their quality is likely to be lower. We have not had much of that trouble because of our standards. Everybody recognizes the Little Theatre in Tulsa as the group where you go to learn something and to do the best work.

GARD: You'd say, then, the Tulsa Little Theatre actually sets the standards for the whole community of living theatre?

VIEHMAN: Yes, and the result is that the city generally places the theatre on a level with the Philharmonic Orchestra and university activities. It's one of the notable institutions of the city.

GARD: I'm right, am I not, in thinking that the Little Theatre is not part of a city-wide plan of integration of art or cultural activities?

VIEHMAN: It has no connection.

GARD: Is there thought in the city of integrating these cultural things?

VIEHMAN: I was talking last night to the man who is chairman of the board of the Philharmonic Orchestra, and we were talking of a plan which is already started but has not gotten very far in the Chamber of Commerce, of having an over-all cultural committee, which I think should become a Tulsa foundation.

In other words, if that kind of civic organization has the proper vitality in individuals and purposes, then the wealthy people who want to make contributions to the arts could have a place to put their contributions—into a foundation. I see that foundation as having a board of such caliber that they can receive appeals from the Philharmonic Orchestra if they get into trouble, or the Tulsa

Little Theatre if they get into trouble, of if the Philbrook Museum needs some money for a new building to expand. The board could appraise these requests and make allotments. I think that is necessary in any city of this size. It has been started, but it's lagging at the present time. We were talking last night about getting a group together to discuss formation of such a cultural committee with a foundation attached.

GARD: We recently established a Wisconsin Arts Foundation and Council for the whole state with something like your whole purpose in mind, in developing these things through a central agency.

VIEHMAN: If you don't do something of that sort at the present stage of our cultural development, you find the various organizations competing with one another.

GARD: Has anyone, so far as you know, ever made a large money grant to the Tulsa Little Theatre?

MRS. VIEHMAN: No, never.

VIEHMAN: As I said a while ago, I'm not sure that's a good thing. We have a Board of Directors at the present time who are very proud of the fact that they have done everything on their own without subsidies.

GARD: Have they actually held back people from making gifts?

MRS. VIEHMAN: No.

GARD: They have never had large sums offered. I see.

VIEHMAN: And I say again, I'm not sure that's right. I think the Tulsa Little Theatre at the present time would be a bigger theatre under proper leadership if, occasionally when they needed it, they had been able to have a subsidy.

GARD: Now I want to come to a couple of questions relating to the operation of the theatre staff—the paid staff. You are, of course, the director. What kind of paid staff do you have?

VIEHMAN: The paid staff consists of the director, an assistant director, who is a full-time man, business secretary, and an assistant box-office woman—four people. There is a part-time janitor, but all the rest of the activities of the theatre are voluntary.

MRS. VIEHMAN: We have about 350 volunteer people actually at work on one play.

GARD: I take it you both agree that volunteer work in Community Theatre is a good or necessary thing. In other words, I'm getting at this problem of the professionalization of the Community Theatre. There are some in the country that are going definitely in that direction, quite away from the volunteer basis on which this was started. Could I have some comment from you about that?

VIEHMAN: My position on professionalization is more or less neutral, I think, or betwixt and between. I believe there are some places where full professionalization is wise, though in professionalizing fully you lose something. You lose the interest of a great many people as volunteers. There's something vital in their interests that makes the theatre of widespread interest to a city.

These 350 people who work with us on one show have their roots in all parts of the city. They and their friends make for general personal interest in the theatre. Of course, a side issue or by-product of such friendship is the improvement of the cultural level of those people who partake. I mean that they get an opportunity to express themselves, to use their imaginations, their initiative. This is possibly very amateur in the very early stages. But a person who has taken part in one show, and is interested, comes to the next show that he takes part in at a higher level of competence, interest, and ability. Those are the advantages of widespread volunteer contributions.

However, volunteer operation also has its disadvantages. When you rely on a volunteer crew to come out some night and you expect to have fifteen people and only four arrive, your whole program gets behind. Now, if your staff was a professional staff or a paid staff, you could lay your plans and follow through on your plans.

The net result of the volunteer system is that the director who sets out at the beginning of the rehearsal with a certain objective and level in mind has to compromise all along the line and do the best that he can with his staff and the people who volunteer. That is the disadvantage of the complete volunteer, amateur system. And it's a big one if you have ideals that you want to attain. You are prevented from reaching those ideals that you may have for any production. So, in the volunteer system, even with a fine imaginative director, the ultimate production is always less than that he sets out to get.

I'm not saying that the same couldn't be true with a professional staff. You make compromises in this creative work everywhere. But the probability is that the director's ideals could be better attained if he had a solid paid staff to do the work. This is one of the areas I think some kind of subsidy to the community would be valuable. That the staff could be enlarged to the point where not so much dependence would need to be put on the volunteer, and where there would be somebody to do the job when the volunteer doesn't show up.

GARD: Are you speaking of acting staff as well as technical?

VIEHMAN: No, not so strongly in acting, but to some extent. As a matter of fact, some of the Community Theatres have sort of merged into a semi-professional system. For instance, the actor is given expense money, and pretty soon that expense money varies. You want one actor badly and you are tempted to give him more expense money than another actor, and as a result you get into all kinds of trouble. I know some theatres that are operating that way at the present time. I have in my group of people here in Tulsa some actors who have appeared fifteen to twenty-five times in various plays. Having worked with some professionals in New York, I would rather have these people in my productions—these home people with their experience and their open minds—than many professional actors. However, here's the problem: I use, in the course of a year, about a hundred actors in our six shows. We don't repeat very often during a season partly because of the home and business time demands on the people and partly because our audience likes to see different faces. So 50 per cent of those actors in a season's time will be completely new to our stage, and some of them new to any stage. When you mix these folks with experienced actors, you have a problem. You have to give the inexperienced ones a good deal more time. The director must go over the same fundamentals on every production in order to keep and get the new people up to the level of the experienced actors, and that is a great disadvantage.

However, in the long run, it keeps your field large from which you can cull people, and as you lose people from your city or they get too busy to work in a play, you get new people to replace them. We have a card index at the present time of about 250 people who have appeared in past plays and we can, and do, call them.

MRS. VIEHMAN: Our audiences have often said that as much as

they enjoy an actor in one production they very seldom want to see him twice in a season. We have real complaints if they see one actor too frequently.

GARD: What theatres in the Southwest do you know of that are actually paying expense money?

VIEHMAN: I don't know of any myself.

GARD: I know the Pittsburgh Playhouse does, but there are none down here?

VIEHMAN: Of course, the Margo Jones Theatre is completely professional. And sometimes these small expense compensations are made and they don't show on the books. But I don't know of a single Community Theatre in the Southwest that operates that way.

GARD: This brings up the subject of leadership in this whole operation of yours. You rely heavily on volunteer people. Obviously some of them have more leadership characteristics than others. Do you make any attempt to pick out and train particular people for leadership roles in your operation?

VIEHMAN: I don't think I should say we make any particular attempt. I think there isn't time for it. When you are putting on a show every six weeks there just isn't time. That happens because as soon as you find a person who handles a job, you just give him more jobs to do and his leadership just comes out naturally. You keep loading him with responsibility as often as he will take it.

GARD: But you have no plan of developing new leaders and a backlog of leadership?

VIEHMAN: No, that would be wonderful, but there isn't the time. Our volunteers work all day and they work on crew or rehearsals every night during the run of the play, and the result is there isn't any time.

MRS. VIEHMAN: There is some attempt, in a very loose way, in some of our committees. I mean, in our Play Choosing and Casting Committee, we try to groom people to take on the chairmanship. It is not an easy job. In the Board of Directors they try each year to find competent people in the city to take responsibilities.

GARD: The Board of Directors is the real leadership of the organization?

VIEHMAN: Our Board of Directors has a rather interesting setup. There are eighteen directors, six of them are elected each year for a three-year term. They are elected by ballot of the membership. The ballot is sent out in June for the Board of Directors for the following year. The Board, when it is organized, selects from themselves their own President, Vice-President, Second Vice-President, Secretary, and Treasurer. All the rest of the Board is appointed, each to be responsible for a field. For instance, one member of the Board is responsible for the organization of a Play Choosing and Casting Committee; one has two or three of the technical branches backstage; one has publicity; one has program; and so on; so that the whole field of the theatre is covered on the Board by supposedly responsible people. They must organize the committees and find the people to do the job. At least, that's the paper layout. It doesn't always work out.

GARD: How much of the real work falls back on you as director?

VIEHMAN: Whenever anybody fails, the director and the assistant director have to fill in and do the job.

MRS. VIEHMAN: We also have to keep check of things and see that the publicity is moving in the right manner; that the right things are emphasized, and to work with the publicity chairman. We've been fortunate in having some very able people. Sometimes, of course, there are some who are not so able.

GARD: Have you ever had a major disagreement or split in the Tulsa Little Theatre? Have there ever been cliques or factions formed that have warred with one another over an issue?

VIEHMAN: Once or twice a near crisis. I've been here only fifteen years of the thirty-five years.

GARD: Can you enumerate any of these small things? They usually seem to be small.

VIEHMAN: The choice of plays and the casting is always something of a problem, but I am protected as director by a clause in my contract which says the choice of plays and the casting of plays must be satisfactory to both the director and the theatre. Now, then, the theatre appoints the Play Choosing and Casting Committee, and if they come up with something, and vote unanimously to do a play, and I would say no, that's the end of that. Or if I say that I would like to do a certain play and the theatre committee says no, that's the end of that, too. In other words, we each have a veto.

Actually, that kind of controversy seldom comes up because

I meet with the committee, they don't meet alone. And we always come to an agreement long ahead of time on the play because we know what will happen if we don't. Only once do I remember when the play that was picked by both the Casting Committee and the director had started rehearsals and the Board raised a fuss about it and wanted to change the play. I agreed to change the play for one that they wanted. The play turned out to be a lemon and it's never happened since.

GARD: What is the percentage of female to male participation? Do you have many more women than men wanting to participate in the actual work of production?

MRS. VIEHMAN: Well, frequently; but I think one of the interesting things about our theatre is that our audience is very well balanced. Once a woman finally talks her husband into going to the theatre, you find the men look forward to the plays as much as the women. As far as participation on stage, I think more women do come around.

VIEHMAN: Backstage in the technical end we have a more or less balanced number of men and women on the make-up committee. We have almost entirely women on prop committee because . . . well, that's obvious. When it comes to building, the building crew and painting crew are probably about equally divided. In sound, it's mixed. Girls work on the switchboard as well as men, so that's pretty well divided. When it comes to acting, you always have more women present themselves than men; but the funny part of it is, I can always get my men cast first. Problems come up in the casting of the women. Actually, the men who present themselves for an acting part, as a rule, are better actors than the general run of the women. I think more idle women with little ability for the job come out as applicants for parts.

GARD: There wouldn't be any justification for saying that the Tulsa Little Theatre was a woman's activity?

MRS. VIEHMAN: Oh, no.

GARD: Then the community regards it as a virile and masculine organization. Tulsa is, after all, not too far from the frontier period. You'd expect the women to carry the cultural burden.

VIEHMAN: As a matter of fact, I've seen this question come up on the Board when they got up a nomination slate: hadn't we better get more women on this Board? There are too many men!

Another thing that has happened in the past six or seven years at membership time in the fall of the year, we usually have a one-act or a scene from a play rehearsed to donate to the Service Clubs in town. The only thing that we ask is that we make a pitch and give them a membership card. For that we give them a performance of that one-act play. It results in getting many men from the Service Clubs to come out and work the front of the house; to come out and act; to learn to know the Little Theatre as more than just another club in town.

Actually, the politically minded men of the Service Clubs come out and want to be in a play to become better known. They appear in a show before 7,000 discriminating people. That's nice publicity.

GARD: Have you ever elected a mayor for Tulsa on that basis?

MRS. VIEHMAN: No, not yet! But the radio, television, and newspaper people all work at our theatre and, of course, the frustrated actors who are now on television and radio come out at the drop of a hat when they can be relieved of time at the station.

VIEHMAN: The Theatre here is regarded by radio and television people in town as a training ground. We seldom have had a production that hasn't had one, two, or three radio or television people in the cast.

MRS. VIEHMAN: The plays run on a very professional stage basis. Our stage manager has been with us for fifteen to twenty years. He's developed a good corps of assistants around him and he's responsible for the operation of the stage. It's not as though Joe comes in to do just this show and Tom comes for the next. They regard it in a really professional manner.

GARD: Do you ever sell out entire performances of your play to any one group?

VIEHMAN: We used to, but not any more. The trouble is now to get our actors to agree to do eighteen performances without a break. (That's our usual run.) We could still sell individual performances, but we don't have control over our actors that much.

MRS. VIEHMAN: The actors loathe playing special performances, too. The club shows were very difficult audiences.

GARD: You say that it's difficult to hold actors for eighteen performances? Are you always able to do it? Are there instances where it can't be done? I'm thinking now, whether it would be easier to do that with a semi-professional company if you were able to pay some actors.

MRS. VIEHMAN: I don't think paying makes that much difference in this town.

VIEHMAN: Well, if you have paid actors, you have all their time. Actually, the eighteen-performance run means times that we can't get certain actors. I give a very clear picture when people come in. At that time, I make an announcement: This play will tentatively open on such and such a date and will play for a minimum of fifteen performances, with a possibility that we may have to extend the run three or four performances. The rehearsals will last four weeks, including three dress rehearsals. We rehearse six times a week— Monday, Tuesday, Wednesday, Thursday, Friday, and Sunday afternoons for a three-hour session and sometimes longer. Now, if you cannot subscribe to that rehearsal and playing schedule, there's no use your reading at all. . . .

In other words, it's very clear in advance. Now it's got to the point where our better actors and the people who enjoy acting set up a certain time when they put everything aside, bridge parties, and so on; and they go to their bosses and say they can't make any out-of-town trips in the next seven weeks, and is that all right? It's set up in advance so they devote that time, which they enjoy and want to do. Then you probably don't get them again that year. That's how it generally works out. The long run still operates against our getting certain actors. Busy people can't give that much time, particularly people who are called out of town.

GARD: Are you doing anything in the community by way of adult education outside the formal theatre program? Do you offer any special lectures, or anything of the sort, to arouse public interest? Do you offer any classes?

VIEHMAN: We have no classes at the present time, but the matter has been in my mind and, to some degree, in discussion for several years. It would be a great advantage to us, regardless of what advantage it would be to the people who took the classes. For instance, if we gave classes in acting and speech, that first work that has to be done with every actor—and that has to be done in the production rehearsals—would be, to some extent, eliminated. However, at the present time, with a staff of two production people, it's impossible. So that remains as an objective to aim at when our staff is increased to the point where we can handle it.

GARD: Well, what's your chief recommendation to the smaller Community Theatre? How could their role be bettered?

VIEHMAN: About three years ago I got a long-distance call from a doctor down in San Angelo, Texas. He said, "I was at one Southwest Theatre Conference meeting and I heard you talk and I wonder if you would come down here and talk to our organization and tell them what you think is wrong with them, and what they could do to get ahead."

They had an organization down there that had struggled along for three or four years with nothing but volunteer directors all along the line. He said he would pay my expenses down—I didn't charge him any fee at all. Gerda and I flew down and we stayed overnight with them. They had a dinner and we talked about the whole setup, and the next year they got enough money together to get a paid director, which was my *first* recommendation. Now they are sailing along beautifully. They just needed some help and it wasn't just money help. Get a paid director is my advice.

GARD: I'd like to have your opinion on two more things. Briefly, what is your attitude here toward the development of local playwrights, local to the region, that is, and the production of their work?

VIEHMAN: First of all, we have had a playwrights' contest here. Gene McKinney of Baylor and John Rosenfield, who is the entertainment editor of the *Dallas Morning News,* were back of it. Gene was chairman of the new-plays contest in the Southwest and John was on his committee. John got a sum of money to be given to the organization that would produce a new play which by a committee of New York judges would be considered the best new play of the area. They conducted that contest for two years, and not a single play turned up that was anywhere near worth producing.

Now, coming back to my personal feelings, I believe strongly that in this American theatre setup we must find a way to encourage new playwrights, because the chance of a man writing his first play and getting it done in New York so that he can learn something is very remote. Where does he get it done? I can't do it here, unless it happens to be a very good first script and happens to have some interest, because a man has been local or known to our audience. I can't do it because my box office goes right down when I announce a new play. The result is that we haven't done a new play in this theatre for a good many years. Now, I do think that the place for the new playwright to get his opportunity to have his play done is in the university theatre. I still think that's the only place left for him to get it done.

MRS. VIEHMAN: I understand even the Margo Jones Theatre is going to have to change their policy. They, too, are having trouble finding good scripts.

VIEHMAN : Their policy for years was to do nothing but classics and new scripts, and they did some of the new scripts that later appeared in New York; but they can't find enough scripts.

MRS. VIEHMAN: Paul Baker at Baylor is doing new scripts at the university. They strongly try to encourage new playwrights in Texas. And Virgil Baker at Fayetteville, Arkansas, is also trying to do new scripts. What is your opinion?

GARD: Well, you know as well as I do that opinions, regarding the responsibility of the Community Theatre to develop and produce new plays, vary exceedingly. To many leaders in American Community Theatre, the area need have little responsibility at all. These leaders argue that new script production rightly belongs to the college theatres, which are subsidized institutions and, therefore, able to take the risks involved. You've just said that. They offer the point of view that the sole responsibility of the Community Theatre is the entertainment of the audience, and that maximum entertainment is more likely to be achieved through the use of "tried and proven" plays, and preferably plays of reputation achieved in New York or London.

On the other hand, a stout body of opinion rests on the other side—the side favorable to new plays.

These proponents of the idea maintain that the level of financial risk is low, especially in comparison with professional casts. They hold that the playwrights of the future will develop in many American places if they receive the proper encouragements. These encouragements include taking the writer in as a part of the group and of

the group's purpose. The group would offer sympathetic understanding and, perhaps, financial assistance if needed. While the
production of new plays might not be a foremost aim, the occasional production of a new script would be considered of tremendous
importance to the group, the community, and to the writer. Indeed,
important to the welfare of the nation.

The fact that more new plays are not produced in Community
Theatre is partly the fault, in fairness, of the writers themselves
and of those who may control their plays.

The evidence is that there are not numbers of new plays of merit
available to Community Theatre directors. The best of the new
scripts are very frequently in the hands of agents of possible professional producers who will seldom permit use of the unproduced
play in a Community Theatre situation. Writers are not yet in the
habit of seeing the Community Theatre as a vital steppingstone to
professional success, and, therefore, they seek a market in New
York.

The Community or local Theatre is perhaps the only great and
widespread way through which new playwriting may flourish.
Howard Lindsay recently told me, "Our great theatre is bound to
be local or regional. It cannot, because of finances chiefly, be otherwise." The attitude toward new plays is at present negative and
non-dynamic. This is motivated by fear of financial failure and a
habit of conformity. Yet the facilities are available throughout
America for the most dynamic and satisfying kind of aid to the playwright . . . the kind that would tend to root him in a center, or
theatre-conscious place. If only Omaha, or Tulsa, or Pittsburgh, or
any of the fine Community Theatres could make new plays a foremost cause.

Perhaps they can't without a certain amount of beginning aid,
or without a certain demonstration somewhere that the new-play
idea is worth while. If the movement caught fire, it might burn
steadily. Everywhere one gets the impression that, though the attitude is negative, with a little added education there might be many
new experiments undertaken. Experimentation with new plays was
not a foreign idea to many of the earlier Community Theatres.
During the art-fermenting days of the twenties, one-act plays were
written which have never been bettered and, indeed, remain as

part of the backbone of short dramatic literature. The idea was to be creative, imaginative. This notion is still around, but it's hard to find.

VIEHMAN: I would probably produce a new play if I found one that wouldn't knock my season in the head.

GARD: Just one more item. You said acceptance of theatre in the community had a direct relationship to the unavailability of commercial theatre.

VIEHMAN: I'm not sure it would be in direct proportion to the availability of professional theatre; but I think it quite true, and you can prove it in many, many cases, that theatre, under proper leadership, will have its strongest growth, its fastest growth, in those regions that are pretty well removed from commercial theatre in any form. But, of course, local theatre has to have personalities to set it off. I mean the people in those districts are not going to suddenly say, "We want theatre—we want theatre." Somebody has to set it off, but the growth will be greatest in those districts where they are not able to see much theatre.

MRS. VIEHMAN: We have a small number of road companies at the present time in Tulsa. And in this town people travel frequently and they see theatre. They come home and say, "I saw the play you are doing at the Tulsa Little Theatre in New York. The production here stood up very well." Sometimes they say ours is better.

VIEHMAN: There is a comparison between the average professional road company and the Community Theatre work. I'm talking about comparing the Community Theatre with good leadership and understanding against the road company of a year or two of age; and I am convinced that there is more freshness and spontaneity, if not technical proficiency, in the better Community Theatre production than there is in the average road company.

Conversation with Mack Scism

Mummers Theatre
Oklahoma City, Oklahoma
Population—290,000

Near the center of downtown Oklahoma City a warehouse has been turned into an arena theatre. In its sprawling, raftered way it has a soul, and the soul of the Mummers Theatre is a young idealist named Mack Scism.

In conversation he speaks quietly, but there is fire behind everything he says. He sees the local theatre as the foremost institution in community life, and he does what he can to make it so for everyone. Artistic integrity would describe his attitude. His comments were pure idealism tempered with practical experience.

GARD: About this subject of your experiences with original plays, have you been experimenting with them ever since the opening of theatre here?

SCISM: No, the first new script was done in 1952.

GARD: What was the script, do you remember?

SCISM: Yes, indeed. It was *Child's Play,* by Florence Stevenson, and concerned the witch hunts in Salem in 1692.

GARD: Please give your absolutely frank opinion about the Community Theatre's responsibility toward the production of new plays by new writers.

SCISM: To get an audience to spend time in the theatre, it is necessary to present something that is not only entertaining but that is thought-provoking. In trying to find plays for one season

121

after another, I have become disheartened by the dearth of really good scripts. The only answer seems to be that we need more playwrights writing better and more beautiful plays.

The Broadway market is limited because of the financial risk involved in undertaking a new script, while our financial risk is very limited. We can produce a play for just a tiny fraction of what it costs to do one in New York. We are not faced with collapse if the new play doesn't happen to be a hit—a hit in that it will have sufficiently good reviews in the papers.

It was a joy for us to have the experience of working with a script that had not been tried. This was a challenge, and the opportunity for our own creativity to come into use is obvious. We have been fortunate enough to have some of the playwrights work with us right here, as we rehearse, and this has led to some of our most exciting experiences.

Happily, every new play we have produced has been a financial and artistic success. We feel that the theatre must do what it can to promote the establishment of a fine dramatic literature in America. The best way to do that is not only to keep alive the best things that have already been written but to encourage new playwrights. The Community Theatres are the very ones to do this.

GARD: Have any of these new writers come from Oklahoma?

SCISM: Not one.

GARD: How interested are you in trying to promote or find talented persons in the locality?

SCISM: Extremely interested. However, when we start looking for a new play, we immediately take on a huge responsibility to the new playwright. We must handle the script with dispatch, and spend much time thinking over what has been read in order to decide whether it is suitable for us to produce. This lack of time is one reason why we have not done a new script for two years. This doesn't mean we don't want to do one, and as soon as it is possible to hire an adequate staff we'll do more about encouraging regional drama.

GARD: How, in theory, would be the best way of helping the playwright?

SCISM: The best thing would be to have an author-in-residence.

From reading new plays it is evident that the new playwright needs most of all to associate with theatre directly.

GARD: Would you like to have a playwright-in-residence if one could be made available?

SCISM: Oh, yes. If a playwright is here and is injected into the theatre's mechanism and can see plays in rehearsal and in performance, even if they're not his own, it would be a help to him in writing a play.

GARD: Would you want to select such a writer yourself, or would you be willing to have a good writer sent here who was relatively unknown to you?

SCISM: It would probably need to be a mutual agreement. That they send someone who is acceptable to us and we agree to take someone who is acceptable to them—the outside agency, that is.

GARD: You wouldn't necessarily have to have a big-name person who could come here? You'd be willing to take a younger person of talent who is struggling along?

SCISM: Certainly. In fact, all the plays that we've done have been just that sort. We've produced no plays by anyone who is well known at all. The only one who—of course, when we did his play he wasn't at all—was, was Theodore Apstein. We did his play, *Illusion,* before it was produced on Broadway. But, for the most part, they have just been young people completely unknown.

GARD: Are there any problems that you haven't mentioned— problems concerned with the production of original plays that you would like to mention?

SCISM: The big problem is if the author is not with you in the revisions that are always necessary—*we mustn't revise the play ourselves because that's the author's job.* And to have to handle that by correspondence slows the whole business down, and some of it never gets done.

Only so much can be done before a play goes into rehearsal. It's very seldom that a new script can be found that has every single line in it absolutely right, and so often there are purely mechanical things that need to be done to the play. The more involved work in character development or scene structure needs the author right on the spot. If he is here to see the situation, the job of working out the problems is much easier.

Conversation with Ramsay Burch

Margo Jones Theatre
Dallas, Texas
Population—434,462

Mr. Ramsay Burch, former director of the theatre founded in Dallas, Texas, by Margo Jones, built solidly upon the original ideas of the founder. It was her idea to start a permanent, repertory, native theatre with a resident staff of the best artists available. This theatre was truly a "war baby," and because of the financial limitations of the forties, had only a paper existence for six years.

Careful planning and boundless imagination permitted purchase of a building on the Fair Grounds for arena-type productions. Accenting the wish of Miss Jones to make the theatre a living, vital, contemporary part of Dallas, the name of the theatre incorporates the current year and advances as the years change; as, for instance, Theatre '59 will give way to Theatre '60.

The philosophy of good theatre has been emphasized with outstanding results by Mr. Burch. High ideals for drama have been consistently applied to the Dallas community, and the resulting productions of the Margo Jones Theatre are examples of real creativity. There has been a concentrated plan to produce classic dramas and the best scripts offered by new playwrights, so that the people of Dallas might have the opportunity to see fine plays done in a beautiful way.

Mr. Burch believes that the higher one aims the farther one can go, and he has illustrated well how ideals may reach practical reality in this playhouse. He believes that security, through continu-

124

ous permanent livelihood, should be offered to actors and technicians to bring from them the best of their creative talents. In Dallas, a loyal supporting citizenry has made this possible.

GARD: Mr. Burch, how long has this theatre been in operation?

BURCH: Ten years.

GARD: And who started it?

BURCH: Margo Jones.

GARD: And it was started as a community project?

BURCH: As a civic non-profit organization. Under our charter we are tax-exempt.

GARD: But you now employ a professional company?

BURCH: That's right—always have.

GARD: What is your opinion of the idea of professionalizing the Community Theatre in America?

BURCH: Well, I think there is room for both the professional theatre and the Community Theatre—that is, what we usually refer to as the "little theatre." We have a Community Theatre right here in Dallas as well as a professional theatre, and I don't say that the little theatre should be made professional any more than the professional should be made nonprofessional.

GARD: You think the employment of actors in American communities is something we ought to be investigating and making plans for?

BURCH: Yes, I certainly do. I think once again we come to that old phrase, "decentralization." Most of our actors seem to gravitate either to New York or the West Coast, and I think we need to develop actors outside both of these areas . . . professional actors.

GARD: What percent of your present company comes from Dallas? That is, do they have their homes here, or are they natives of the city?

BURCH: At present none, although from time to time we have had professional actors from Dallas here, and we supplement our company from time to time with equity actors. Many of these actors have started out with us doing bit parts, and have eventually grown and become professional through us. We try more and more to develop local talent, because, after all, it saves us transportation and gives us a pool of talent right here.

GARD: Do you do anything to develop your local talent other than your regular theatre program? Do you conduct any kind of classes?

BURCH: No, we have no classes. Actually, with our schedule, one play every three weeks playing in the evening and matinees, we need to devote all our attention to the production. It is pretty difficult to hold any outside courses of any kind.

GARD: Now, I'd like to ask you two or three questions about the financial side of your operation, if you don't mind. This theatre has always been pretty much in the black as far as its operation is concerned, hasn't it?

BURCH: Yes, I would say generally speaking. There have been minor deficits at times, and that's where our Board of Directors comes in. If we run into a small deficit, they usually come to our rescue, but it's never been of any major proportion.

GARD: This theatre is really operated then by a Board of Directors. How many people are on the Board? Are they what you might call upper-income citizens of Dallas?

BURCH: Approximately forty people serve on the Board. Yes, we have some upper-bracket people and we have some of moderate or middle class—I use that term as far as financial status is concerned. But we select those who are interested in theatre and in the various arts and who co-operate by contributing their services in other ways than just contributing money.

GARD: Your company is paid on an equity basis. It's a full equity company, in other words. The director is employed and a technical director, and who else?

BURCH: Technical director and assistant technical director, property man and a stage manager. That is our technical crew.

GARD: And the people who attend your plays, are they, would you say, of any one income level in the community, or is it a fair cross-section?

BURCH: No, we definitely get a cross-section.

GARD: What are your ticket prices? What's your top price?

BURCH: Evenings, all one price—three dollars. We have a great many season ticket holders, of course, and when they buy season tickets we reduce the price to $2.50 for the evening performances.

GARD: What is the price of your season ticket?

BURCH: Twenty-two-fifty for the nine shows.

GARD: The theatre then, in general, has never been badly in debt nor is it in debt at the present time? A thing that has interested me in a few places has been the personality of an instigator or developer of a Community Theatre. I guess everybody knows that most significant art developments come out of idealistic, dynamic, or talented personalities. This theatre, I understand, was developed by Margo Jones. Has her disappearance from the scene made a noticeable difference in the attendance at plays, or in the general acceptance of the theatre in the community?

BURCH: No, it hasn't. Fortunately, Margo had this theatre for six years, no, seven years, before she died, and it became so well established on a national basis through its policy of doing new scripts and classics that it's almost become a part of the community now, and I haven't noticed any decrease in interest. Of course, when we do a good play, there's always interest. If the play is bad, like any other theatre, the interest decreases.

GARD: What has the attendance been, for instance, for *Uncle Vanya,* which you have in production now?

BURCH: I'd say it's been a little below average.

GARD: Even the people in Dallas have to be educated to the classics.

BURCH: Yes, with one or two exceptions. We find that Shaw and Shakespeare, and sometimes even Molière, will attract more business. We get crowds for Shakespeare and Shaw, particularly from students. Perhaps, due to the fact that Chekhov is more advanced, we haven't had as many students. I imagine that is because Chekhov is not widely studied in high school.

GARD: In your general aims and purposes of this theatre, do you have any organized intent to raise the standards of appreciation in the community by producing a certain number of classics during a year's season?

BURCH: It has always been the policy to produce two or three classics during the season and just hope!

GARD: And do you think your hope, in general, has been justified?

BURCH: Yes, yes, it has. As I say, particularly some classics are more popular than others.

GARD: Now, I know that this theatre has always been interested in production of original plays and the encouragement of new writers. Do you want to make any comment about the importance of that in a community of this size?

BURCH: Well, I think it's important in a community of any size. Margo's idea was that there would be no theatre without the writer and, of course, we all have to agree with that. When this theatre was started there were not nearly as many off-Broadway theatres doing what this theatre has been trying to do. In other words, this theatre is a pioneer in the policy of doing unproduced scripts by untried authors. We have done at least seventy-six original scripts. Many of these have gone from here to Broadway or to England for English productions, or they have been picked up by publishing companies, such as Samuel French.

GARD: Do you want to make any comment about the prestige value of the production of original plays, insofar as the theatre itself here is concerned?

BURCH: Well, I think original plays have helped the prestige of this theatre a great deal. We have done such originals as Tennessee Williams' *Summer and Smoke* and William Inge's *Farther Off from Heaven,* when these playwrights were comparatively unknown. And we are still doing plays by playwrights who may become famous in a few more years. Yes, I think that it does help the prestige. Of course, often we do scripts that, as far as audience appeal is concerned, may be classfiied as "flops." However, we think there is something in doing the script to encourage the playwright and to give him an opportunity to see his play in rehearsal. Therefore, we have to take those chances and sometimes we deliberately do so because that's our policy.

GARD: Does your attendance go up or down when you do an original play?

BURCH: If an original play is a hit, it goes way up. For instance, when we did *Inherit the Wind,* we did tremendous business. We have had other successful plays. It doesn't seem to matter whether the play is new or old. It depends on the public and critical reaction to it.

GARD: Most people think that the term "original play" is anathema to the Community Theatre and they refuse to pay much attention, or have very much to do with it at all. Your advice to Community Theatre directors, then, would you say, is to pay more attention to good original plays?

BURCH: I would read all the original scripts that I could possibly get. Of course, you have to read an awful lot before you find one you think is worth producing, but the effect in searching is worth while, I believe.

GARD: If you had the money, what would you do that you are not doing now?

BURCH: There would be several things that we could do. I've always wanted a larger resident acting company than we have, but because of our seating capacity limitation it's difficult to have a larger company. Our actors have been working for the same salary for ten years. I've wanted to raise salary, but we are limited here, as you can see. We seat only 198 people. It doesn't matter if we have a hit and people are clamoring at the doors, we still can get only a limited number of people in here. Therefore, we have to watch our budget very carefully.

I would like to investigate the possibility of getting better and more new scripts. I would love to be able to go abroad and get some foreign scripts, for example, that have never been produced here. We could do so many things that I can't even begin to enumerate, if we had additional funds.

Really, our one particular *immediate* project is finding new scripts. That is major in itself, and takes an enormous amount of reading and an enormous amount of time. The major intent and purpose of this theatre is to find new scripts and to encourage new playwrights. With more money we could do a better job.

GARD: As far as you know, your location will continue to be here in the State Fair Park?

BURCH: No, sir, we hope not eternally.

GARD: You'd like to move if you could?

BURCH: We would like to move to a more modern, slightly larger, and, perhaps, a little differently designed arena theatre. This building was not primarily constructed for arena theatre. It has been converted, and there are many, many improvements needed.

GARD: Do you use any volunteer helpers at all in connection with the production of plays, or in ticket campaigns, or anything of the sort?

BURCH: No. We do use what you might call volunteer actors occasionally. When we have a large cast—when we do a Shakespearean production, for example—our resident company won't take care of it, so we get people who are interested in acting for the mere love of acting. However, we don't use any volunteer labor in the theatre work or the season ticket drive . . . that's usually our own Board of Directors. They're volunteer labor, of course, but they have an interest.

I would like, someday, to see this theatre be a year-around operation instead of its now thirty-week operation. What we need is a more permanent resident company. Now we have actors coming and going. One reason is that we can't pay them too much. The television and movie offers are tempting, and they can make much more money elsewhere. In other words, if I could get a nucleus of a company that would remain and work year after year for a number of years, I think we could develop a group in the tradition of, say, the Abbey Theatre or the Old Vic. Now we have a constant turnover; and just when we begin to know the actor, he leaves.

GARD: What do you, in most ideal terms, think the theatre in the community ought to be?

BURCH: In the first place, public participation, I think, is our greatest problem. When I say public participation, I really mean public interest. The theatre needs to do all that it can to break the conventional molds, raise the levels, do things that are different from things people see every day on television or in the movies. We have to decide whether what we do is going to be art or commercial theatre.

I think it's up to every Community Theatre to decide whether they are going to repeat the Broadway hits, the proven things that they know are going to go, or whether they are willing to break that mold and do some original things. To get some original ideas will make people think and start people talking about the theatre and make them know that in the theatre they can see something different from anything, any place.

Conversation with Theodore Sizer

Fort Wayne Civic Theatre
Fort Wayne, Indiana
Population—133,607

Fort Wayne is an arts-conscious city. It is an American community bent on doing some constructive work in behalf of the arts. A Fort Wayne Fine Arts Foundation is a real community force that has actually helped to lift community arts high above the average. The common man in Fort Wayne has excellent opportunity to see good local theatre; to hear good music locally performed; to be exposed to a variety of experiences in the visual arts.

In the fabric of the Arts Foundation the Civic Theatre is important. Its director is dedicated to the production of a high-quality bill. Theodore Sizer, Director when Fort Wayne was visited, is a thoughtful man—an idealist. He is slender, wears glasses, speaks fluently.

GARD: How long has the Civic Theatre been operating in Fort Wayne, Mr. Sizer?

SIZER: This is its twenty-sixth season. It has had the history of most Community Theatres. It began with people being interested in doing plays in the twenties after the road died; and they rehearsed in schools, banks, and offices; and presented two or three plays a year. Ainsworth Arnold was the first director. Other directors were hired, or at least engaged, for each production. However, in the thirties, 1933 or 1934, the Majestic Theatre became available to the group and, through the efforts of some of the members who were

131

interested in it, the building was obtained. It is an old, regular, big theatre. It has wonderful facilities and was built just a little over fifty years ago. It was primarily built, of course, for touring company groups, and there is little area for rehearsal and for shops, but it has a very fine stage—forty-five feet deep and seventy feet wide— and a very pleasant auditorium. It had been used for many productions, including *Ben Hur,* and great stage people crossed its boards, they say. During the twenties and thirties it fell into disrepute and even became a burlesque house, so it was saved when purchased by the Civic Theatre.

The first name was The Old Fort Players, and then, when they took over the theatre and remodeled it, they changed the name to the Fort Wayne Civic Theatre. It's had several prominent directors like Lyle Hagen and Newell Tarrant. I have only been here for the last four years, but the theatre is a well-established one. It has a large body of community supporters and actors, and during the years it has developed a staff of four people including the director, technical director, business manager, and secretary.

GARD: How many people does your house seat?

SIZER: Well, at present it seats about seven hundred. We do not usually fill it.

GARD: How many performances of a play do you generally do?

SIZER: Well, we do at least six performances, and then we have houses which are bought out for a certain price by organizations, and sometimes we will run as high as thirteen or fourteen performances.

GARD: Do you sell subscriptions at the beginning of the season?

SIZER: Yes, we do.

GARD: How much are these?

SIZER: The downstairs seats are ten dollars for the season. Upstairs we sell at seventy-five cents per seat, and we charge five dollars for a season subscription.

GARD: Now, I know that there is in Fort Wayne a relationship of the arts under the Fort Wayne Fine Arts Foundation, and the Community Theatre is a member of this Foundation. Now how does this all work out, in your most honest and candid opinion? Are you in favor of this kind of merging of the arts in the community? Does it help the patronage of the Community Theatre?

SIZER: Well, I don't see how it could not help. Personally, I am very enthusiastic about the Fine Arts Foundation. I would like to think that I am one of the important cogs in this organization, because ever since I have been in this city it has been a cherished plan of some people, but now it has moved recently into a concrete thing, and I feel that it is an important aspect of our whole cultural life. The Community Theatre, the Philharmonic, and the Art School are all members of this organization, as well as the Fort Wayne Ballet and the Historical Society. This city is described by many people as the most happy city in the country, because so many of the people, when questioned here recently, said that they would rather stay in this city than move away. The children particularly, because they found so many fine activities in the city. And I think that Fort Wayne in many ways has all of those factors which make it really a typical American city.

I know that when big advertising people want to check on a product they check Fort Wayne, and if the response here is reasonable, then it's assumed that it will be good all over the United States. So I think in many ways this city offers a typical situation. Fortunately, I do think music, art, and theatre here are on a very high level.

GARD: Would you say, then, that the patrons of the theatre represent a pretty good cross-section of the Fort Wayne population?

SIZER: I could hardly say that it's a cross-section. I would say that of those in the city who have a broad education (and there are many here who have a college background because of the demand of the industries), that there are a lot of people who are interested. I doubt if we can expect a lot of the lower middle-class income folk to be enthusiastic supporters, but I am sure the theatre will have an effect upon their life gradually. I think it's having effect among the professional and the upper-middle class. There are a great many people who are becoming more and more interested in theatre and more keenly interested in seeing something fine happen with theatre here.

GARD: Could you say that people who attend the theatre are apt to also attend the Philharmonic?

SIZER: Oh, yes, we find that many of our Board members overlap, and many of our memberships overlap. We don't conflict on dates, so that we find we don't compete time-wise. There is in every community what I would call a "hot nucleus" . . . people who support and work on the committees of every art aspect, and we find them almost interchangeable. If they are not at the art school, they probably are working at the theatre.

GARD: Now, about taste in the community, so far as the kind of plays the community wants and will accept. Are you able to do classics with success here?

SIZER: Yes, I think we do them very successfully. We do one Shakespeare a year. In the last four years we've done *A Midsummer Night's Dream, The Merchant of Venice, Macbeth,* and *Henry IV— Part I.* We also did *Murder in the Cathedral,* doing it not only on the stage at the theatre but also in two of the larger churches.

GARD: Are you allowed to do any play that you want to do, regardless of what the subject matter may be?

SIZER: I could do that or we could do that, but I do feel that there are some plays which would not be, let's say, happily received. We always get letters from some group or individuals who feel that our play choice was bad. However, I do not believe that we should do certain types of plays lest we disturb a large group of people. It's a matter of taste. We have a large play-reading committee who consider all the plays that are available, not only the current ones, but also the classics.

This is a church city—and there are a great many people here closely connected with churches, and so I do ask the ministers and the church association to give me some advice, although I am not pressured at any time into doing any particular kind of play.

GARD: It's fine that you have an agreeable Board of Directors.

SIZER: They agree with the program; however, we ask the audience for a vote. Right now we are asking them what plays they would like to see next season. We have submitted twenty plays and the audience is voting on them. This will help guide us in selecting. Actually, they have voted very heavily for such plays as *Glass Menagerie, The Little Foxes, Anastasia,* and many other plays which I think are of a very high caliber, with, incidentally, a strong vote for *Hamlet* and *Twelfth Night.*

GARD: You need strong actors to do those plays. Do you look forward to professionalizing the Fort Wayne Civic Theatre?

SIZER: The fault with using the professional in our position in the theatre is that we cannot tell exactly where the line of the professional begins and the amateur ends. The difference between the amateur and the professional is not the *pay* but the *skill,* and this is a very subtle thing and can hardly be measured. I do sometimes think that we should invite professional actors to come and perform with us. However, we then get into problems with the local stagehands union and with other organizations. So, frankly, I do not feel that the amateur theatre, at least in Fort Wayne, can afford to have professionally paid actors as part of their staff, or as part of their organization. If we did as many plays as some organizations do, well then, perhaps we would have to consider it. At the present time the supply of actors and the number of people who want to do volunteer work is sufficient, and we have developed many almost professional people as far as skill is concerned. We find that we have no difficulty even in doing Shakespeare because there is a particular group who usually do Shakespeare and they have developed great facility.

GARD: What, in your opinion, does the Community Theatre need most?

SIZER: Well, many Community Theatres are very badly housed and many of them need professional directors. Actually, the professional direction part of it, as far as the staff is concerned, is extremely important. I think a Community Theatre is like a YMCA, the Public Library, or any institutional type of activity. The essential thing is to get a staff and a building in which people can work. You have an atmosphere to create, and that is exactly where the confusion often occurs. So often show business is confused with the theatre. And I don't think in the community that that's what you want. What you do want is an atmosphere and situation that make it possible for a great many people to participate. You need a theatre where you can create magic and have people enjoy it in a real theatrical atmosphere.

GARD: I take it you believe, as I do, that the establishment of playhouses in the community as symbols of the living theatre is extremely important.

SIZER: I do, indeed!

Conversation with Jules Irving

Actors Workshop
San Francisco, California
Population—775,357

Jules Irving is intensely sensitive—an idealist. He is Drama Director of San Francisco State College and earns a portion of his living there. He is, however, best known as the co-founder of the nationally famous Actors Workshop. Irving's sights are high—the plays experimental and done with great creativeness. In 1958, the Actors Workshop was selected as the community group to represent America at the Brussels World's Fair. In conversation he is eager, seizing ideas quickly and with intense interest. The Actors Workshop produces in the Marines' Memorial Theatre in downtown San Francisco.

GARD: Mr. Irving, when was The Actors Workshop in San Francisco started?
IRVING: In January, 1952.
GARD: And it has gone continuously since then?
IRVING: Yes, with nary a letup in five years.
GARD: And is it a professional company?
IRVING: At the moment we have a contract with Actors' Equity, the Stagehands' Union, the Musicians' Union, House Management Union, so I guess from all standpoints we would be considered professional; although we are categorized as what might be called the off-Broadway company, inasmuch as there are compromise arrangements with each of the guilds. I might say this, that despite

136

the fact that we put a great many long hours into our work we have not achieved sufficient financial security at the moment to warrant all our people earning their basic livelihoods in the theatre.

Consequently, all of us earn our livelihoods doing something else and spend our off hours working at the theatre. So we are not professional in that we earn our complete living from it. We hope to someday.

GARD: Who directs your productions?

IRVING: The productions are usually directed by Dr. Herbert Blau, who is my associate, and myself. We've produced something close to twenty-four productions. Dr. Blau has produced about half and I have produced half of them, and in three instances we had three other directors direct for us.

GARD: Do you have a fairly stable company in the sense that about the same people work with you all the time?

IRVING: Originally, in 1952, we started with nine members, and of those nine members six are still with us after a period of five years. Another fifteen members joined us the first two years of operation, and they are still with us. I would say that the nucleus of the company has remained intact. There is the usual turnover that one might find in most noncommercial companies.

GARD: Do you rent the playhouse you are in?

IRVING: We are on a lease arrangement with the Marines' Memorial Theatre management, yes.

GARD: Is the company at present in any serious indebtedness, or are you operating in the black?

IRVING: I'm very happy to say that we are operating in the black at the moment. We've paid all of our debts, which were vast over a number of years; but during the past year, when we first started our first subscription season, the company became completely solvent.

GARD: Do you have any idea about what your budget is per year for operation?

IRVING: I'm just guessing now, but I think in our last annual accounting period we spent approximately $55,000.

GARD: Now, what is the philosophy of your company? Do you have any definite aim or purpose?

IRVING: I think that basically I can say the aim and objective of

our company is to produce that dramatic literature which is worth
while of representation, and which poses an artistic challenge to the
artists involved in the theatre. I think we wish to make some contribution to the community in terms of an expression on the part
of a playwright.

We are interested in any playwright, provided that what he has
to say seems to be significant and meaningful to a community such
as San Francisco. We don't subscribe necessarily to any individual
philosophy of playwriting. We believe that our theatre is dedicated
to producing worth-while theatre, exciting and dynamic theatre,
which provides entertainment for the audience.

However, I think it's reasonable to say that that entertainment
rests in a kind of dramatic literature which is meaningful rather
than what might be termed frothy or strictly commercial. I think,
in a humble way at least, we've been able to prove that the so-called
"noncommercial" theatre, if it is produced on a high artistic level,
will be marketable at the box office.

GARD: Can you give me a couple of examples of the kinds of
things you mean?

IRVING: We have produced within the last five years Ibsen's *Hedda
Gabler,* Sophocles' *Oedipus Rex,* Tennessee Williams' *Camino Real,
The Girl on the Via Flaminia;* and one of our big successes was
Arthur Miller's *The Crucible.* We produced Strindberg's *Miss Julie,*
and *The Plough and the Stars.* One of our recent successes was the
delightful comedy, *The Flowering Peach,* by Clifford Odets. Currently we are producing Samuel Beckett's *Waiting for Godot.*

GARD: You think the people respond to the kind of theatre that
you are giving them. In other words, your audiences have increased?

IRVING: Well, in 1952, we started with an invitation audience of
some fifty people for our first production, at which we charged no
admission at all. We produced a second and a third show, and went
on subscription. We had very little publicity and a fairly uncomfort-
able theatre. We started in a room above the judo academy, and
over the period of time we've increased that original audience of fifty
until recently we played *The Flowering Peach* to over a thousand
people. We have over nine hundred season subscribers at the
moment, so that within five years our audiences have very defi-

nitely grown in a very encouraging manner. We feel there's a good future for the theatre in San Francisco.

GARD: How many nights do you play?

IRVING: At the moment we only play two nights a week, Friday and Saturday, in a 640-seat house. I might say that when Miss Viveca Lindfors was with us, which was the first time we tried the star system, we did play seven nights a week and one matinee. San Francisco did accept that.

GARD: Now, could you make a comment about the worthwhileness of professionalization of Community Theatres? What is your opinion?

IRVING: I think this is an extremely important factor in the theatre. We have within our ranks some of the finest young actors— not only in San Francisco but, I think, in the entire country. I think of two or three individuals in our company who have had very excellent training and originally had aspirations of going to the New York theatre since this was the only place one could earn a livelihood in the theatre, but had very serious doubts about the nature of the theatre being produced in New York.

They thought there was very little emphasis upon the artistry of the theatre, very little emphasis on the playing in which you have a togetherness of a group of people working on a play, so that the very tightness of the group actually sells the play and makes the play exciting. This is the kind of theatre which is not possible in New York—which is pretty much on the stock-market gamble system in which a company of actors are corraled together for a four-week period and then, after the show closes, they work with other people.

We have very little opportunity in our country for what we call the "ensemble theatre." And, as a result, some of these young people who have come with us have given up the idea of going to New York simply because they have found a great deal of satisfaction in expressing themselves in this kind of theatre in a craftsmanlike and artistic manner. They find they have made a contribution to the community, and have had more or less of a settled life— with the single factor missing at this point, that is, the actor is not able to earn his living at his art but must work at a department store during the day. One of our young men, Bob Simonds, works in a fruit market from one in the morning until eight in the morning so that he can support his wife and two children and yet be free to express himself in the theatre. At this moment, a chap like Bob Simonds earns from the Actors Workshop the ridiculous sum of $7.50 a week, which takes care of minor expenses.

I think that a part of his artistry actually suffers because the boy is tired. He's playing the lead in *Godot* now, and it takes a great deal of energy for him to do this. One of our dreams is to reach the point where we can assemble a nucleus of actors who will work exclusively in our theatre. I might also add that I think this is extremely important insofar as what a truly American national theatre would be. We have tended not to develop what might be called an American style of acting simply because we have not developed groups such as Ireland's Abbey Theatre, or such as the many group theatres that are seen on the Continent. We don't have an ensemble company in America, and I think that if we were to lose our people, people such as Bob Simonds and many of our other actors, to the Broadway theatre—which is the only theatre at which they can earn a living—I think it means a great loss to the American theatre in terms of what we have attempted to develop here in San Francisco, at least. That's the reason I think professionalism is essential.

GARD: I didn't get quite clear exactly how much your present company is professionalized.

IRVING: Well, we have an agreement with Actors' Equity which says that in a company of eleven or more we must have five full equity people. That means that these are full members of the union who earn a maximum salary of thirty dollars a week, depending upon the number of performances. In a cast of ten or less we are required to have three equity people. Within our company we do have a ruling that, whenever the box office warrants it, at least the expenses of the equity and non-equity members are shared. We also have a ruling, because of the size of our company, that members must be in residence with the company at least two years before they earn the right to draw their expenses.

GARD: Could I ask you now what you think of the encouragement of the playwright in the community? Are you interested in finding playwriting talent on the West Coast?

IRVING: Oh, very, very anxious. We have read easily over a hundred scripts in the past year—not only from this area but from all over the country. We are extremely anxious to find original material that we can produce at the theatre. We are doubly anxious to find playwrights in the area who may be cultivated. Again, there are just so many things an organization such as ours can do because of time. We do all our work after hours, from seven in the evening on, and weekends. All of us, as I have said before, earn our living during the day. As a result, the playwright has been somewhat neglected simply because of lack of time, and, again, this is something we think professionalization would help us solve.

GARD: Your company is administered by the company itself. You have no Board of Directors from the community?

IRVING: No. Dr. Blau and myself started this company on a corporate basis in which we retain complete control of the company on an undemocratic basis—primarily because we felt that democracy in the theatre was rather a cumbersome way of operating. We have found that our actors, who have no say in the administration of the company, are actually content not to have the administrative responsibility. Dr. Blau and myself have assumed all those responsibilities ourselves, and as a result there is no Board of Directors. We maintain the policy, the play selection, the casting, the business administration, and, of course, we are subject to a certified public accountant.

GARD: Now, do you have any ideas what an outside agency might do for your company? Have you any needs that aren't being met at the present time by your present level of income? Any ideas you have as to how you might improve your work if you had additional funds?

IRVING: Well, I think that the thing I mentioned before, that time is of the essence. The mere fact that we are not able to support our people so that they can put in a full eight-hour working day in the art of the theatre, I think, hinders us from reaching a complete and full fruition or realization of an aim, goal, or an ideal.

I have always believed in a subsidization of some kind and have been extremely anxious to get it. We have always felt that the Opera has never been expected to support itself, the Symphony hasn't been expected to support itself, nor the Art Museums, but yet the theatre

is expected to support itself. I think we have clung tenaciously to
the ideal that a successful theatre must be a sound financial enterprise as well as an artistic entrprise, and we have remained solvent,
but pretty well by the skin of our teeth because so many corners
must be cut and the first person to suffer, unfortunately, is the actor
because of his time. You start rehearsal at seven at night and it
must break at ten-thirty or eleven at the latest, because he must get
to work early in the morning. There is just so much that can be
done in a limited rehearsal schedule. It means that a full realization
of one's objectives can't be reached and, as a result, you become
somewhat frustrated. The greatest help must be really to the actor.

GARD: So you would use funds, if you had them, to improve and
make available more time from your acting company?

IRVING: Yes, I would want to see that actors earn a livelihood
at the theatre rather than elsewhere. And, in addition, I think there
are any number of specific projects which have challenged us and
again have been set aside because of lack of time. One of the things
we have always been interested in is the establishment of an
Academy of the Theatre in San Francisco. In our company we have
a great many people who teach at universities and colleges, who
have a very firm background in educational theatre and the training
of the actor in voice and diction and movement, acting techniques,
playwriting, and dramatic structure. We've had a great many requests from people to start a school because many of the people
who work in our company have grown as a result of their affiliation
with these fine theatre craftsmen. Again, because of lack of time
and funds, we have not been able to establish such an academy,
and this is another thing I think we would do if we had funds
available.

GARD: Do you do anything with children's theatre?

IRVING: Yes, we have, and this is another project. I've been
interested in children's theatre for the past five years and have
produced seven children's theatre productions. I write the scripts
myself, my wife and I. We do them as original musical comedies
and tour them for the San Francisco Children's Theatre Association and for the Peninsula Children's Theatre Association twice a
year. They are completely original scripts designed from our shop
and, again, this is another project I have been encouraged on (but

funds have kept me from fully realizing it) . . . to set up a touring company of children's theatre to bring the productions which have been extremely well received and reviewed to a great many other areas in northern California. Lack of funds prevents me from doing this, of course.

GARD: This is theatre acted by adults for children, right?

IRVING: Yes.

GARD: Now, is there anything else you think is unique about your company that you would like to say something about—something I haven't asked you?

IRVING: Well, of course, I feel very strongly about the objectives of the company and the people in it because I have been receiving almost a dozen letters a week from actors in New York who have heard of the company in one way or another. I've been very gratified at the kind of reputation the company has. People who have come through San Francisco, I think, have been somewhat taken, and I say this in all humility and objectivity, with the quality of the work, considering the circumstances under which we do operate, and as a result I've had a vast number of actors requesting permission to come to San Francisco to work with the company.

My answer has always been, because I don't want to disillusion them, that there is no opportunity here for actors to earn their living in the theatre. And, I might say, not only actors, for I really didn't pay enough attention to theatre craftsmen. We have great and fine designers in San Francisco as well as potential playwrights, as well as theatre technicians, all of whom must work in the not-strongly-supported-enough Community Theatre so they can earn a living from it. In terms of these actors in New York, I have been discouraging them simply because there is no opportunity for them to work; and yet a great many of them have answered my discouraging letter with a plea for permission to come out and work for nothing simply because they feel that dedication to the ensemble and to the particular kinds of plays that we have done seems somewhat unique in our country, and that having dedicated ourselves to this kind of theatre we are rather gratified that we have at least been accepted in San Francisco to the point where, at least, we are in the black even on this level of operation.

Bibliography

ALLEN, HERVEY. *Israfel.* New York: Farrar & Rinehart, Inc., 1934.

ARVOLD, ALFRED G. *Little Country Theatre.* New York: Macmillan Company, 1922.

BARTON, JOSEPH E. *Purpose and Admiration.* New York: Frederick H. Stokes & Co., 1943.

BENTLEY, ERIC. *The Dramatic Event.* New York: Horizon Press, Inc., 1954.

———. *In Search of Theatre.* New York: Alfred A. Knopf, Inc., 1953.

BLAKE, BEN. *Awakening of the American Theatre.* New York: Tomorrow Publishers, 1935.

BOSANQUET, BERNARD. "Croce's Aesthetic." (Proceedings of the British Academy). London: 1919-20.

BOURNE, JOHN. *Actors by the Thousand.* New York: Longmans, Green and Co., Inc., 1944.

———. *Drama Festivals.* London: Sir Isaac Pitman & Sons, Ltd., 1939.

BROWN, ROLLO WALTER. *The Creative Spirit.* New York: Harper and Brothers, 1925.

BROWNELL, BAKER. *Art Is Action.* New York: Harper and Brothers, 1939.

BURLEIGH, LOUISE. *The Community Theatre.* Boston: Little, Brown and Co., 1917.

BUTLER, GEORGE D. *Introduction to Community Recreation.* New York: McGraw-Hill Book Co., Inc., 1949.

CHENEY, SHELDON. *The Art Theatre.* New York: Alfred A. Knopf, Inc., 1917.

———. *The New Movement in the Theatre.* New York: Mitchell Kennerly, 1914.

145

CHENEY, SHELDON. *The Theatre.* New York: Longmans, Green and Co., Inc., 1929.

COGGIN, PHILIP A. *The Uses of Drama.* New York: George Braziller, Inc., 1956.

Community Drama. Playground and Recreation Ass'n of America. New York: The Century Co., 1926.

CONNELLY, MARC. *The Arts in Renewal* (an essay). Philadelphia: University of Pennsylvania Press, 1951.

CRAIG, EDGAR GORDON. *On the Art of the Theatre.* Boston: Small, Maynard & Co., 1924.

————. *The Theatre Advancing.* Boston: Little, Brown and Co., 1919.

DEAN, ALEXANDER. *Little Theatre Management for Community and School.* New York: D. Appleton & Co., 1926.

DEWEY, JOHN. *Art as Experience.* New York: Minton, Balch & Co., 1934.

DEGOVIA, C. J. *The Community Playhouse.* New York: B. W. Huebsch, Inc., 1923.

DICKINSON, THOMAS H. *The Case of American Drama.* New York: Houghton Mifflin Company, 1915.

————. *The Insurgent Theatre.* New York: B. W. Huebsch, 1917.

————. *An Outline of Contemporary Drama.* New York: Houghton Mifflin Company, 1927.

DOLMAN, JOHN, JR. *The Art of Play Production.* New York: Harper and Brothers, 1928.

DRINKWATER, JOHN. *Art and the State.* Liverpool: 1930.

Encores, or Successful Community Theatre Leadership. Pittsburgh: Carnegie Institute of Technology Press, 1948.

ERVINE, ST. JOHN. *The Organized Theatre.* New York: Macmillan Company, 1924.

FEIBLEMAN, JAMES K. *Aesthetics.* New York: Duell, Sloan and Pearce, Inc., 1949.

FREEDLY, GEORGE, and REEVES, JOHN A. *A History of Theatre.* New York: Crown Publishers, Inc., 1955.

GARD, ROBERT E. *Grassroots Theatre.* Madison, Wisconsin: University of Wisconsin Press, 1955.

GASSNER, JOHN. *The Theatre of Our Times.* New York: Crown Publishers, Inc., 1954.

GLOVER, HALCOTT. *Drama and Mankind.* Boston: Small, Maynard & Co., 1924.

GREEN, PAUL. *Drama and the Weather.* New York: Samuel French, Inc., 1958.

———. *Dramatic Heritage.* New York: Samuel French, Inc., 1953.

HAIGH, A. E. *Attic Theatre.* Oxford, England: Clarendon Press, 1927.

HANDLER, NATHALIA. Thesis, University of Wisconsin, 1954.

HARTNOLL, PHYLLIS. *The Oxford Companion to the Theatre.* London: Oxford University Press, 1951.

HASTINGS, CHARLES. *The Theatre.* London: Duckworth and Co., 1901.

HENDERSON, ARCHIBALD. *Pioneering a People's Theatre.* Chapel Hill: University of North Carolina Press, 1945.

HOPKINS, ARTHUR. *Reference Point.* New York: Samuel French, Inc., 1949.

HOUGHTON, NORRIS. *Advance from Broadway.* New York: Harcourt, Brace & Co., 1941.

HUGHES, GLENN. *History of the American Theatre 1709-1950.* New York: Samuel French, Inc., 1951.

IRVING, SIR HENRY. *Theatre in Relation to the State.* London: E. H. Bacon, 1898.

ISAACS, EDITH JULIET RICH. *American Theatre in Social and Educational Life.* National Theatre Conference. New York: 1932.

———. *Essays on the Arts of the Theatre.* Boston: Little, Brown & Co., 1927.

JONES, HENRY ARTHUR. *Foundations of a National Drama.* New York: George H. Doran Company, 1912.

JONES, MARGO. *Theatre in the Round.* New York: Rinehart & Co., Inc., 1951.

LANGFELD, HERBERT SIDNEY. *The Aesthetic Attitude.* New York: Harcourt, Brace & Co., 1920.

MACCARTHY, DESMOND. *Theatre.* London: Oxford University Press, 1955.

MACGOWAN, KENNETH. *Footlights Across America.* New York: Harcourt, Brace & Co., 1929.

———. *Theatre of Tomorrow.* New York: Boni & Liveright, 1921.

——— and MELNITZ, W. *The Living Stage.* New York: Prentice-Hall, Inc., 1955.

MACKAYE, PERCY WALLACE. *Civic Theatre in Relation to the Redemption of Leisure.* New York. Harper and Brothers, 1912.

———. *Community Drama.* New York: Houghton Mifflin Company, 1912.

McCleery, Alfred, and Glick, Carl. *Curtains Going Up.* New York: Pitman Publishing Corp., 1939.

Mitchell, Roy. *Creative Theatre.* Rahway, New Jersey: Quinn & Boden.

Moody, Richard. *America Takes the Stage.* Bloomington: University of Indiana Press, 1955.

Morris, Lloyd. *The Story of the American Theatre.* New York: Random House, Inc., 1955.

Nicoll, Allardyce. *The Development of the Theatre.* New York: Harcourt, Brace & Co.

———. *The Theory of Drama.* New York: Thomas Y. Crowell Co.

Noyes, Carleton. *The Gate of Appreciation.* New York: Houghton Mifflin Company, 1907.

Patten, Marjorie. *The Arts Workshop of Rural America.* New York: Columbia University Press, 1937.

Parkhurst, Helen. *Beauty, An Interpretation of Art and the Imaginative Life.* New York: Harcourt, Brace & Co., 1930.

Peacock, Ronald. *The Art of Drama.* Lewans Mead, Bristol: The Burleigh Press, Ltd., 1957.

Pearson, Talbot. *Encores on Main Street.* Pittsburgh: Carnegie Institute of Technology Press, 1948.

Pendleton, Ralph. *The Theatre of Robert Edmond Jones.* Middletown, Conn.: Wesleyan University Press, 1958.

Phelps, Wm. Lyon. *The Twentieth Century Theatre.* New York: Macmillan Company, 1918.

Pichel, Irving. *Modern Theatre.* New York: Harcourt, Brace & Co., 1925.

Quinn, Arthur Hobson. *History of the American Drama from the Civil War to the Present Day.* Vol. I. New York: Harper and Brothers, 1927.

Reynolds, Ernest. *Modern English Dramas.* Norman: University of Oklahoma Press, 1949.

Roenheim, Richard. *The Eternal Drama.* New York: Philosophical Library, Inc., 1952.

Rolland, Romain. *The People's Theatre.* Translated by Bassett H. Clark. New York: Henry Holt & Co., 1918.

Samachson, Dorothy and Joseph. *Let's Meet the Theatre.* New York: Alfred Schuman, 1954.

Saylor, Olive M. *Our American Theatre.* New York: Brentano's, 1923.

———. *Revolt in the Arts.* New York: Brentano's, 1930.

SCHNEIDER, ELIZABETH. *Aesthetic Motive.* New York: Macmillan
Company, 1939.
SCHOEN, MAX. *Enjoyment of the Arts.* New York: F. Hubner &
Co., Inc., 1944.
SELDEN, SAMUEL. *Man in His Theatre.* Chapel Hill: University of
North Carolina Press, 1957.
SPER, FELIX. *From Native Roots.* Caxton, Idaho: Caxton Press,
1948.
STEVENS, THOMAS WOOD. *The Theatre from Athens to Broadway.*
New York: D. Appleton & Co., 1932.
WORK, WM. Thesis, University of Wisconsin, 1952.

A Representative List of American Community Theatres

(arranged by states)

ALABAMA

BIRMINGHAM
Town & Gown Civic Theatre
2131 Sixth Avenue

FLORENCE
Tri-Cities Community Theatre

GADSEN
Little Theatre of Gadsen
P.O. Box 901

HOMEWOOD
Valley Theatre

HUNTSVILLE
Little Theatre of Huntsville

MOBILE
Joe Jefferson Players, Inc.
P.O. Box 1504

Mobile Theatre Guild
11 South Carlen Street

TUSCALOOSA
Tuscaloosa Little Theatre

ALASKA

ANCHORAGE
Anchorage Little Theatre, Inc.
P.O. Box 96

ARKANSAS

FORT SMITH
Fort Smith Little Theatre

ARIZONA

COOLIDGE
Coolidge Little Theatre

DOUGLASS
Douglass Little Theatre

PHOENIX
Phoenix Little Theatre

TUCSON
Tucson Little Theatre

150

CALIFORNIA

ALAMEDA
Alameda Little Theatre

ALPINE
Alpine Players
Route 1, Box 304

ARCATA
Arcata Community Players

AUBURN
Auburn Community Theatre
Placer College

BERKELEY
Berkeley Little Theatre Workshop
2211 Grove Street

Company of the Golden Hind
P.O. Box 225

The Good Hope Company

CHICO
Chico Community Little Theatre
P.O. Box 968

COVINA
Covina Little Theatre

EAST BAY CENTER FOR THE
 BLIND
The Lamplighters
3834 Opal Street

GRASS VALLEY
Golden Drama Guild

HAYWARD
Hayward Community Theatre

HUNINGTON
Hunington Park Civic Theatre
City Hall

LA JOLLA
Drury Lane Community Players,
 Inc.
Box 997

LONG BEACH
Long Beach Community Playhouse

MARYSVILLE
Yuba-Sutter Players
Yuba College

MENLO PARK
Menlo Players Guild

MENTONE
The Footlighters

MILLBRAE
Millbrae Community Players

MONTEREY
California's First Theatre

OJAI
Theatre Branch of the Com.
 Art Center
P.O. Box 331

OXNARD
Little Theatre of the Oxnard
 Evening School
Oxnard Evening School
5th and H Streets

PALO ALTO
Palo Alto Community Theatre

PITTSBURG
Pittsburg Community Theatre
 Guild
City Hall

PORTERVILLE
The Barn Theatre

CALIFORNIA (cont.)

REDDING
Redding Little Theatre

REDWOOD CITY
El Camino Players

ROSEVILLE
Spotlite Productions

ROSS
Ross Valley Players

SACRAMENTO
Sacramento Civic Repertory
1419 H Street

SAN BERNARDINO
The Playmakers

SAN CARLOS
San Carlos Community Theatre
City Hall

SAN DIEGO
Footlights Theatre

Pastime Players Playbox

San Diego Community Theatre
P.O. Box 2171

SAN FRANCISCO
Actors Workshop

The Interplayers
Municipal Theatre

San Francisco Community
  Theatre
3119 Fillmore Street
The Shadow Players
745 Buchanan Street
Theatre Arts Colony
1725 Washington Street

SAN MATEO
Peninsula-Hillburn Little
  Theatre
Box 543

SANTA ANA
Santa Ana Community Players

SANTA BARBARA
Alhecama

STOCKTON
Stockton Civic Theatre

SUNNYVALE
Sunnyvale Little Theatre
334 Sunnyvale Avenue

TRACY
Tracy Community Players

VALLEJO
Mira Little Theatre Guild
614 Alabama Street

WHITTIER
Whittier Community Theatre

COLORADO

BOULDER
Boulder Community Players

COLORADO SPRINGS
Civic Players of Colorado
  Springs
Box 383

GOLDEN
Golden Thespians
City Hall

LAKEWOOD
Lakewood Community Theatre
  Assoc.
P.O. Box 7713

LAS ANIMAS
Las Animas Little Theatre

PUEBLO
Pueblo Civic Players
625 West 19th Street

CONNECTICUT

HARTFORD
Mark Twain Masquers
P.O. Box 787

MANCHESTER
Community Players
Manchester Center Thespians
Center Congregational Church

NEW HAVEN
Nutmeg Community Theatre
YWCA Howe Street

WATERBURY
Waterbury Civic Theatre
P.O. Box 55

WINSTED
The Footlight Club, Inc.

DELAWARE

ARDEN
Players Guild of Arden

CHESTERTOWN
Chester Players

EASTON
The Easton Players

NEWARK
University Drama Group

WILMINGTON
Wilmington Drama League
Y Players

DISTRICT OF COLUMBIA

WASHINGTON
Arts Club
2017 Eye Street

Calvary Guild Hall Players
Calvary Methodist Church
1459 Columbia Road, N.W.

Employee Activities Program
W.S. Department of Agriculture
Room 1071, South Building

Foundry Players
500 16th Street, N.W.

Mount Vernon Players
9th & Massachusetts Avenue,
N.W.

Theatre Lobby, Inc.
17 St. Matthew's Court, N.W.

The Thespian Study Club
1717 Otis Street, N.E.

Unitarian Players
All Souls Church Unitarian
15th & Harvard Streets, N.W.

FLORIDA

ANNA MARIA ISLAND
Island Players

CLEARWATER
Francis Wilson Memorial
302 Seminole Street

DAYTONA BEACH
Daytona Beach Little Theatre
P.O. Box 2359

DELAND
Deland Players, Inc.
Shoestring Theatre
P.O. Box 54

FLORIDA (cont.)

DELRAY BEACH
Delray Beach Players, Inc.
Box 1827

FORT LAUDERDALE
Fort Lauderdale Little Theatre
P.O. Box 320

FORT MYERS
Fort Myers Little Theatre

GAINESVILLE
Gainesville Little Theatre, Inc.

HOLLYWOOD
Little Theatre of Hollywood
Box 1561

JACKSONVILLE
Arlington Players
2001 Chaseville Road

LAKE WORTH
Lake Worth Playhouse
Box 784

LAKELAND
Lakeland Little Theatre
Box 129

MIAMI
Country Club of Coral Cables
    Theatre Group

The Civic Theatre of Greater
    Miami

MOUNT DORA
Icehouse Players, Inc.

ORLANDO
Community Players, Inc.
Old Chapel Building, Old Air
    Base

PANAMA CITY
Panama City Little Theatre
380 Bunker's Cove Road

PENSACOLA
Pensacola Little Theatre
E and Intendencia Streets

ST. AUGUSTINE
Little Theatre of St. Augustine
Box 1134

ST. PETERSBURG
St. Petersburg Little Theatre

SARASOTA
The Players of Sarasota

TALLAHASSEE
Tallahassee Little Theatre
Box 3262
North Monroe Street Station

TAMPA
Tampa Little Theatre
P.O. Box 124

VENICE
Venice Little Theatre

WEST PALM BEACH
Norton Gallery Players

WINTER HAVEN
Winter Haven Community Play-
    house
P.O. Box 1499

GEORGIA

ALBANY
Albany Little Theatre

ATLANTA
Atlanta Civic Theatre
P.O. Box 362

AUGUSTA
The Augusta Players, Inc.
647 Broad Street

COLUMBUS
CFA Players

DALTON
Dalton Little Theatre

LA GRANGE
La Grange Little Theatre

MACON
Macon Little Theatre
P.O. Box 449

MOULTRIE
Moultrie Little Theatre

NEWMAN
Newman Players
Dunaway Gardens

ROME
Rome Little Theatre

SAVANNAH
Little Theatre, Inc.

SMYRNA
Smyrna Little Theatre
117 Pretty Branch Drive

HAWAII

HONOLULU
Honolulu Community Theatre
Ruger Theatre

IDAHO

BOISE
Boise Little Theatre

IDAHO FALLS
Idaho Falls Community Theatre,
   Inc.
P.O. Box 106

REXBURG
Upper Valley Community
Theatre

ILLINOIS

ALTON
Alton Little Theatre, Inc.

ARLINGTON HEIGHTS
Village Theatre, Inc.

AURORA
The Lamplighters
642 Lafayette Street

BLOOMINGTON
The Community Players

CHICAGO
Aldelphia Players
Loyola Park
1233 Greenleaf Avenue

ILLINOIS (cont.)

Beverley Theatre Guild
Ridge Park
96th & Longwood Drive

Chase Park Theatre Guild &
Chase Park Footlighters
Chase Park
Leland & Ashland

Chicago Heights Drama Group
1213 Orchard Drive
Chicago Heights

Community Theatres of the Chicago Park District
425 East 14th Boulevard

Globe Players
Avondale Park
3516 School Street

Globe Players & Pulaski Park
Players
Pulaski Park
Blackhawk & Noble

Gold Dome Players
Garfield Park
100 North Central Park

Hamilton Harlequins & Hamilton High School Players
72nd & Normal Boulevard

Institute Players
Jewish Community Centers

LaFolette Community Theatre
& Teen Time Drama Guild
LaFolette Park
Hursch & Laramie

Lithuanian Theatre

Metropolitan Players
64 East Van Buren

Palmer Players
Palmer Park
111 & Michigan

Palos Village Players
1730 West 105th Place

Revere Theatre Guild
Paul Revere Park
2509 Irving Park Road

Riverside Players
River Park
6100 North Francisco

Studio Players
Garfield Park
100 North Central Park

Uptown Circuit Players, Inc.
1040 West Grand Avenue

CHILLICOTHE
The Village Players

DANVILLE
Red Mask Players, Inc.

DECATUR
Decatur Little Theatre & Guild
255 North Main

DEKALB
The Stage Coach Players

DES PLAINES
Des Plaines Theatre Guild

DIXON
Dixon Community Players, Inc.

DOWNERS GROVE
Downers Grove Civic Theatre

ELGIN
Elgin Little Theatre

FREEPORT
Winneshiek Players, Inc.
1227 West Stephenson

GENEVA
The Playmakers, Inc.

HINSDALE
Hinsdale Village Players
30 First Street

JOLIET
"Y" Players

KANKAKEE
Kankakee Theatre Guild

LA GRANGE
La Grange Highland Players

LINCOLN
Lincoln College Community
    Players

LOMBARD
Elmhurst Community Theater
51 North Lincoln Avenue

MATTOON
Mattoon Community Theatre,
    Inc.

MAYWOOD
Maywood Teen-Age Players
Maywood Recreation Depart-
    ment

NAPERVILLE
Naperville Community Theatre

NEW BOSTON
New Boston Theatre Guild

OAK PARK
Oak Park Players

PALATINE
Palatine Players

PARIS
Paris Players

PARK FOREST
Park Forest Playhouse
54 Hemlock Street

PEORIA
Peoria Players
209 Jackson

PRINCETON
State Communtiy Players

ROCKFORD
Rockford Civic Theatre, Inc.
121 South Prospect Street

SKOKIE
Skokie Players

SPRINGFIELD
Springfield Theatre Guild
101 East Lawrence

ST. CHARLES
St. Charles Little Theatre

WAUKEGAN
Waukegan Civic Players
Waukegan Recreation Program

WESTERN SPRINGS
Theatre of Western Springs

WHEATON
Wheaton Drama Club

WILMETTE
Wilmette Little Theatre Assn.
    Inc.
Box 201

INDIANA

CLARKSVILLE
Clarksville Little Theatre Co.,
  Inc.
Montgomery Ave. & Clark Blvd.

CRAWFORDSVILLE
Crawfordsville Dramatics Club

FORT WAYNE
Fort Wayne Civic Theatre

INDIANAPOLIS
Athenaeum Turner Theatre
401 East Michigan Street

The Booth Tarkington Civic
  Theatre

JASPER
Little Theatre of Jasper

LA PORTE
La Porte Little Theatre Club

MICHIGAN CITY
Theatre of Nations
International Friendship
  Gardens

MOUNT VERNON
Hoop-Pole Players, Inc.

MUNCIE
Muncie Civic Theatre
602 North McKinley

NEW CASTLE
New Castle Civic Theatre, Inc.

NOBLESVILLE
Community Theatre

RICHMOND
Richmond Civic Theatre
18 North 6th

SOUTH BEND
Presbyterian Players
P.O. Box 932

TERRE HAUTE
Community Theatre of Terre
  Haute

WHITING
St. John Drama Club
St. John the Baptist Catholic
  Church

WINCHESTER
Randolph Country Little
  Theatre

IOWA

BOONE
Boone Little Theatre

BURLINGTON
Players Workshop

CEDAR FALLS
Cedar Falls Players

CEDAR RAPIDS
Cedar Rapids Community
  Theatre

CHARLES CITY
Charles City Little Theatre, Inc.

CLINTON
Presbyterian Players
First Presbyterian Church

DES MOINES
Des Moines Community Playhouse
831 42nd Street

FAIRFIELD
Fairfield Women's Club Little
  Theatre
300 North Court

KEOKUK
Keokuk Little Theatre
YWCA

MASON CITY
Mason City Little Theatre

MT. PLEASANT
College Civic Theatre
Iowa Wesleyan College

MUSCATINE
Muscatine Community Players

OTTUMWA
Ottumwa Little Theatre
YWCA

SIOUX CITY
Sioux City Community Theatre
416 Thirteenth

WEBSTER CITY
Webster City Community
  Players

KANSAS

COLBY
Little Theatre of Colby

HUTCHINSON
Hutchinson Little Theatre

TOPEKA
Topeka Civic Theatre, Inc.
Box 893

WICHITA
Wichita Community Theatre
110 South Battin

KENTUCKY

COVINGTON
Catholic Theatre Guild
Bush & Washington

LEXINGTON
Guignol Theatre

LOUISVILLE
Clarksville Little Theatre
The Playhouse

MIDDLEBORO
Little Theatre

LOUISIANA

ALEXANDRIA
Alexandria Little Theatre

ALGIERS
Algiers Little Theatre
2529 General Meyers Avenue

BATON ROUGE
Baton Rouge Little Theatre, Inc.
115 St. Louis Street

CROWLEY
Crowley Little Theatre

LAKE CHARLES
Lake Charles Little Theatre
308 Bilbo Street

MONROE
Little Theatre of Monroe, Inc.
P.O. Box 868

NEW ORLEANS
Gallery Circle Theatre

Le Petit Theatre du Vieux Carre
616 St. Peter

LOUISIANA (cont.)

New Orleans Community
　Theatre
P.O. Box 8021

Nord Delgado Barn Theatre
1000 Rampart Street

WDSU-TV Playhouse
520 Royal Street

SHREVEPORT
Shreveport Little Theatre
812 Margaret Place

The Spotlighters, Drama Club
Barksdale Air Force Base

MAINE

LEWISTON
Community Little Theatre Corp.
P.O. Box 904

PORTLAND
Playhouse
Corner Stevens Ave. & Brentwood Street

MARYLAND

ANNAPOLIS
Colonial Players
Community Service Council

Naval Academy Women's Club
　Drama Group

BALTIMORE
Actors' Colony
Jewish Educational Alliance

Club Road Playhouse

The Curtain Callers

Fellowship Theatre
The Baltimore Fellowship

Govans Players
Govans Women's Club

Greek-American Dramatic Club
"Thespis"

IZFA Drama Workshop
Inter-collegiate Zionist
　Federation of America

Ramsay Street Players

Spotlighters
Chizuk Amund Youth Center

The Stagecrafters
Bureau of Recreation

St. James Players

Vagabond Arena Theatre

The Valley Players

Witson Players

"Y" Community Playhouse
YM-YWHA

BETHESDA
Montgomery Players, Inc.
Box 5724

CHESTERTOWN
Chester Players

DUNDALK
Alamedians

EASTON
The Easton Players

ELKRIDGE
Footlight Players

FREDERICK
Community Players

GLEN BURNIE
The Community Players

HAGERSTOWN
Potomac Playmakers

KENSINGTON
Kensington Players
Box 144

LEONARDTOWN
St. Mary's County Little Theatre

RUXTON
Ruxton Players

SALISBURY
Community Players, Inc.

TOWSON
Loch Raren Players
County Recreation Department

MASSACHUSETTS

ARLINGTON
Arlington Friends of Drama, Inc.
P.O. Box 2

BELMONT
Belmont Dramatic Club
490 Pleasant Street

BOSTON
Boston Catholic Theatre
153 Arlington Street

Clarendon Players
1092 Commonwealth Avenue

Field & Forest Club of Boston
30 Huntington Avenue

The Little Theatre Workshop
5 Commonwealth Avenue

COHASSET
Cohasset Dramatic Club
Box 225

FITCHBURG
Amateur Workshop, Inc., of
  Fitchburg
60 Wallace Avenue

LYNN
Tavern Players, Inc.

MIDDLEBORO
Little Theatre Group of Middleboro

MILTON
The Milton Players
P.O. Box O

NEW BEDFORD
The Spouters
P.O. Box 319

Your Theatre of New Bedford
75 Hillman Street

NORWELL
North River Community Club,
  Inc.
Box 395

QUINCY
Community Players of Quincy
51 Edwards Street

READING
Quannapowitt Players
Hopkins Street

ROXBURY
Sidewalk Theatre Players
11 Windsor Street

MASSACHUSETTS (cont.)

WALPOLE
Walpole Footlighters

WALTHAM
Hovey Players, Inc.
Unity Hall
740 Main Street

WAYLAND
Vokes Players, Inc.

WEST MEDWAY
Medway Players

WESTON
First Parish Friendly Society

WEYMOUTH
Brainwey Players

WINCHESTER
Parish Players
First Congregational Church

WORCESTER
First Baptist Church

MICHIGAN

ALLEGAN
Allegan Community Players

ANN ARBOR
Ann Arbor Civic Theatre
P.O. Box 87

BATTLE CREEK
Battle Creek Civic Theatre
P.O. Box 40

BAY CITY
Bay City Players
1500 Marquette

BENTON HARBOR
Twin City Players, Inc.
161 East Main Street

BIRMINGHAM
The Birmingham Village Players
752 Chestnut Street

CLINTON
Clinton Civic Players
11700 Adrian Road

FLINT
Flint Community Players, Inc.
P.O. Box 104

GRAND RAPIDS
Grand Rapids Civic Theatre
24 Ransom Avenue, N.E.

GROSSE ISLE
The Islanders

JACKSON
Jackson Theatre Guild
211 South Jackson

KALAMAZOO
Kalamazoo Civic Players
329 South Park

MARSHALL
Marshall Civic Theatre

MIDLAND
The Midland Little Theatre
  Guild
501 Larkin

MUSKEGON
Greater Muskegon Civic Theatre Assoc.
1336 Sanford Street

OAK PARK
Ridgedale Players
8501 West Ten Mile Road

PLYMOUTH
Plymouth Theatre Guild
Veterans Memorial

PONTIAC
Master Players, Inc.
142 Wayne Street

SAGINAW
Community Playhouse
805 North Hamilton

MINNESOTA

BRAINERD
Pine Bech Playhouse

DULUTH
Duluth Playhouse
12 East Avenue & Superior
  Street

MINNEAPOLIS
Edyth Bush Little Theatre

ROCHESTER
Rochester Civic Theatre, Inc.
Seventh Street, N.W.

MISSISSIPPI

GREENWOOD
Greenwood Little Theatre

JACKSON
Little Theatre Players of Jackson
P.O. Box 245

McCOMB
Pike Little Theatre

NATCHEZ
Natchez Little Theatre

PASCAGOULA
Paspoint Little Theatre
P.O. Box 507

VICKSBURG
Vicksburg Little Theatre

MISSOURI

INDEPENDENCE
White Masque Players

JOPLIN
Joplin Little Theatre

KANSAS CITY
Resident Theatre
1600 Linwood Boulevard

University Playhouse
5100 Rockhill Road

KIRKWOOD
Kirkwood Theatre Guild
P.O. Box 3754

NEOSHO
Neosho Little Theatre

SEDALIA
Sedalia Community Playhouse

SPRINGFIELD
Springfield Little Theatre
316 South Avenue

ST. JOSEPH
St. Joseph Community Theatre,
  Inc.

ST. LOUIS
Community Playhouse, Inc.
812 North Union Boulevard

The Y Players
Downtown YMCA
1528 Locust

MONTANA

MILES CITY
The Barn Players, Inc.
North 12th Street

MISSOULA
Missoula Community Theatre

NEBRASKA

FREMONT
Fremont Community Players

LINCOLN
Circlet Community Theatre, Inc.
1314 Rose Street

OMAHA
Omaha Community Playhouse
4004 Davenport

SCOTTSBLUFF
Platte Valley Community
　　Theatre

SHELBY
Village Players

NEVADA

LAS VEGAS
Las Vegas Little Theatre
P.O. Box 415

RENO
Reno Little Theatre
P.O. Box 2088

NEW HAMPSHIRE

CONCORD
Concord Community Players

EXETER
Exeter Players

HUDSON
Hudson Players

KEENE
Keene Light Opera Co.

PLYMOUTH
Livermore Theatre

NEW JERSEY

ATLANTIC CITY
Toy Theatre Workshop
16 North Essex Avenue

BERNARDSVILLE
Village Players, Inc.
15 Bernards Avenue

BLOOMFIELD
The Footlighters of Bloomfield
Box 406

BORDENTOWN
Bordentown Community Players
15 Walnut Street

BOUND BROOK
Foothill Play House, Inc.

BURLINGTON
Woodside Playcrafters
Community Center

CALDWELL
Playcrafters of Caldwell
Women's Club of Caldwell

CHATHAM
Chatham Community Players

CRANFORD
Cranford Dramatic Club
9 Sylvestre Street

DOVER
Dover Little Theatre
West Elliott Street

EAST ORANGE
Little Theatre of the City of East
 Orange
City Hall

ENGLEWOOD
Jewish Community Center Little
 Theatre
153 Tenafly Road

FAIR LAWN
Radrock Dramatic Group
Box 687

FANWOOD
The Philathalians, Inc.

FLORENCE
Neighborhood Players

FLORHAM PARK
Florham Park Players

GLEN RIDGE
Glen Ridge Players
25 Hawthorne Avenue

HACKETTSTOWN
Town Players

HADDONFIELD
Plays and Players, Inc.

HADDON HEIGHTS
Village Playbox

JERSEY CITY
Emory Drama Guild
Emory Church Parish Hall
140 Belmont Avenue

LEONIA
Players Guild of Leonia

LINDEN
Linden Community Theatre
1408 Summit Terrace

LIVINGSTON
Livingston Little Theatre

MADISON
Green Door Players
James Hall

MAPLEWOOD
The Strollers, Inc.

MARTINSVILLE
Martinsville Community Club
 Players

MEDFORD LAKES
Log Cabin Playhouse

MERCHANTVILLE
Merchantville Playcrafters
Collins Hall

MIDDLESEX
Foothill Play House
Beechwood Extension

MILLINGTON
Lackawanna Travelers
Old Mill Road

MONTCLAIR
Studio Players of Essex County
14 Alvin Place

MOORESTOWN
Moorestown Community Players

MORRISTOWN
Morristown Little Theatre, Inc.
P.O. Box 728

NEW JERSEY (cont.)

MOUNTAIN LAKES
Mountain Lakes Dramatic Guild

MOUNT HOLLY
Holly Group Players
Box 250

MOUNT TABOR
Mount Tabor Theatre Guild

NEWARK
The Center Players
Huld Hall, 652 High Street

Sayre Hall (YWCA)
53 Washington Street

ORADELL
Bergen County Players

PACKANACK
Packanack Players

PLAINFIELD
The Parish Players
First Unitarian Society

Proscenium Players, Inc.

Temple Players of Plainfield
Temple Sholom
West 7th Street

PRINCETON
Princeton Community Players
    Club
59 Bayard Lane

RADBURN
Radburn Players
Grange Hall
Fairlawn Avenue

RIDGEWOOD
Joe Jefferson Players, Inc.
P.O. Box 359

RIVERTON
Footlight Players of Palmyra

ROSELLE
Theatre Guild of the Roselles
119 West 6th Avenue

TRENTON
Spring Street Playhouse
261 Spring Street

UNION
The Revelers of Union, Inc.
1059 Jeanette Avenue

VINELAND
Little Theatre of Vineland
Blvd. at Sherman Avenue

WATCHUNG
The Valley Players, Inc.
Valley Road

WESTFIELD
The Community Players
1000 North Avenue

WOODBRIDGE
Adath Israel Players
Woodbridge Community Center

WOODSTOWN
Curtain Call Club

WYCOFF
The Village Players, Inc.

NEW MEXICO

ALBUQUERQUE
Community Players
Little Theatre

Sandia Base Little Theatre

LAS CRUCES
Teatro Chico

Los Alamos
Los Alamos Little Theatre

Roswell
Roswell Little Theatre
P.O. Box 767

Santa Fe
Corallie Players

Sante Fe Little Theatre

Taos
Taos Little Theatre

NEW YORK

Amsterdam
Amsterdam Little Theatre
24 Guy Street

Ardsley
Ardsley Players

Auburn
Auburn Community Players

Baldwinsville
Baldwinsville Theatre Guild

Batavia
Batavia Players, Inc.
Box 56

Bay Shore
Bay Shore Players
P.O. Box 415

Bellport
Gateway Theatre

Binghamton
Binghamton Civic Theatre, Inc.
53 Nolan Road

Brewster
Little Theatre Group

Brooklyn
Brooklyn Masque Players
504 Hegemon Avenue

Brownville
Brownville Little Theatre

Candor
Candor Community Players

Cazenovia
Cazenovia Little Theatre

Corning
Corning Workshop Players
Corning Library

Cortland
Cortland Community Players
22 Court Street

Croton-on-Hudson
Croton Players

Dobbs Ferry
Dobbs Ferry Woman's Drama
Group

Dunkirk
Dunkirk-Fredonia Players
316 Main Street

East Aurora
Aurora Players, Inc.

East Hampton
Guild Hall Players

East Rockaway
East Rockaway Little Theatre

Elmira
Elmira Little Theatre
P.O. Box 761

Endicott
Suquehanna Players, Inc.

Forestville
Forestville Players Club

NEW YORK (cont.)

FREEPORT
The Curtain Callers

GARRISON
Highlands Drama Workshop

GENESEO
Geneseo Community Players

GENEVA
Geneva Players

GLEN COVE
Neighborhood Players Guild

GLENS FALLS
Glens Falls Operetta Club
Glens Falls Senior High School

GLOVERSVILLE
The Footlighter Civic Theatre

GRANVILLE
Granville Community Players

GREAT NECK
Community Theatre of Great
Neck
142 Baker Hill Road

GROTON
Groton Community Players

HAMBURG
Hamburg Little Theatre

HEMPSTEAD
Little Theatre Workshop
40 McDonald Street

HORNELL
Hornell Civic Theatre
Hornell Public Library

HUDSON
Claverack Players, Inc.
113 Warren Street

HUNTINGTON
Township Theatre Group, Inc.
Box 458

ILION
Ilion Little Theatre Club

ITHACA
Ithaca Community Players, Inc.
P.O. Box 12

JAMESTOWN
Little Theatre of Jamestown, Inc.
Box 675

JOHNSTOWN
Colonial Little Theatre, Inc.

KINGSTON
Coach House Players
12 Augusta Street

LARCHMONT
Larchmont Temple Players
Larchmont Temple

Shoe String Players
5 Locust Ridge Road

LEVITTOWN
The Village Green Players
Levittown Hall

LITTLE FALLS
YMCA Little Theatre Group

LYONS FALLS
The Players Guild
The Playhouse

MAMARONECK
Fenimore Players, Inc.

MAYFIELD
Mayfield Community Players

MIDDLETOWN
Middletown Players Club, Inc.
P.O. Box 132

MONTICELLO
Sullivan County Drama Workshop

NEW YORK
The Amateur Comedy Club
150 East 36 Street

Blackfriars of New York, Inc.
316 West 57 Street

Choreographer's Workshop
471 Park Avenue

Community Players
40 East 35 Street

Everyman's Theatre
152 West 42 Street

Lenox Hill Neighborhood Assoc.
331 East 70 Street

The Lighthouse Little Theatre
111 East 59 Street

Oval Players
c/o S. Holland
271 Avenue C

The Playhouse, YM & YWHA
92nd & Lexington Avenue

The Sixty-Third Street Players
YMCA 5 West 63 Street

NEWBURGH
Newburgh Civic Theatre, Inc.
P.O. Box 45

NIAGARA FALLS
Niagara Falls Little Theatre, Inc.
23 Thomas Street

Northville Community Players
NORTHVILLE

OGDENSBURG
Cathedral Players

OLEAN
Little Theatre Guild of Olean,
Inc.

ONEONTA
Leatherstocking Playhouse
108 Clinton Street

ORIENT
Playshop

OSWEGO
Oswego Players

PELHAM MANOR
Community Theatre Guild

PERRY
Perry Players

PLATTSBURG
Plattsburg Little Theatre

PORT JEFFERSON
North Shore Players, Inc.

PORT WASHINGTON
The Play Troupe of Pt. Washington

POUGHKEEPSIE
IBM Footlighters
IBM Country Club

Vassar Temple Players
Vassar Temple

PULTNEYVILLE
Pultneyville Players

ROCHESTER
Paddy Hill Players, Inc.
167 Johnson Road

Pittsford Summer Theatre
14 Whalin Street

Rochester Community Players
820 Clinton Avenue

NEW YORK (*cont.*)

Spencer Ripley Players

ROME
Rome Theatre Guild & Rome
  Civic Theatre
219 Dominick Street

RYE
Rye Players
51 Milton Road

SAYVILLE
Sayville Musical Workshop, Inc.
P.O. Box 487

SCARSDALE
Port Hill Players

SCHENECTADY
Jewish Center
Community Center

SCHENEVUS
Schenevus Little Theatre

SEA CLIFF
Town Troupers

SLINGERLANDS
Slingerlands Community Players
Box 7-A

SNYDER
Amherst Players
Snyder 21

SPENCEPORT
Ogden Players

SPENCER
Spencer Players

STATEN ISLAND
Dongan Hills Players
Dongan Hills

SYRACUSE
Gilbert & Sullivan Operetta
  Guild

Park Players
Electronics Park

TANNERSVILLE
Onteora Playhouse
Onteora Club

TROY
The Ilium Players
191 River Street

Little Theatre
Dramatics Association

R. P. I. Players
Rensselaer Polytechnic Institute
c/o English Department

TUCKAHOE
Turkeyhoe Players of St. John's
  Church

UTICA
Mt. Carmel Players Guild
649 Jay Street

The Players
47 Ridge Road

Theatre Workshop, Inc.
1020 Mason Street

WALLKILL
Wallkill Footlight Club, Inc.

WALTON
Interim Players

Walton Little Theatre Group

WATERTOWN
Little Theatre of Watertown, Inc.

WAVERLY
Valley Players
Community Center
Sayre, Pa. (Center)

WEBSTER
Webster Theatre Guild

WELLSVILLE
Nancy Howe Players
Public Library

WESTBURY
Westbury Community Players
Memorial Library
Post Avenue

WESTFIELD
Westfield Players

WHITE PLAINS
Dramatic Guild

Masque Players, the Community
    Theatre of White Plains
P.O. Box 95

YONKERS
Community Theatre
117 Park Avenue

Chesterfield Players
St. John's Church

YORK
York Opera Association

NORTH CAROLINA

ASHEVILLE
Asheville Community Theatre,
    Inc.

BREVARD
Brevard Little Theatre

CHARLOTTE
Little Theatre of Charlotte
501 Queen's Road

DURHAM
Durham Theatre Guild, Inc.

GASTONIA
Gastonia Little Theatre, Inc.

GREENVILLE
Greenville Little Theatre Guild

HENDERSONVILLE
Hendersonville Community The-
    atre
Box 1141

HIGH POINT
High Point Little Theatre
Box 1322

KINSTON
Kinston Community Theatre

MONROE
Monroe Little Theatre

MORGANTOWN
Morgantown Little Theatre

NEW BERN
New Bern Little Theatre
Recreation Center

RALEIGH
Raleigh Little Theatre, Inc.

SANFORD
The Little Theatre
Box 588

SHELBY
Shelby Little Theatre, Inc.

WILMINGTON
Thalian Hall

WILSON
Little Theatre of Wilson

WINSTON-SALEM
The Little Theatre of Winston-
    Salem

NORTH DAKOTA

FARGO
Fargo-Moorhead Community
Theatre

OHIO

ADA
Ada Community Theatre
c/o Mrs. Cora Anne Cost
208½ Gilbert Street

AKRON
Center Theatre Guild
Akron Jewish Center

Coach House Theatre
Akron Woman's Club

Community Theatre YWCA
Weathervane Community Playhouse

Wingfoot Players
Employees Activities Office
Goodyear Tire & Rubber Com-
pany

AMHERST
Amherst County Workshop
Players
320 Jackson Street

ASHLAND
Ashland Civic Theatre
220 Ryndale Avenue

ASHTABULA
Ashtabula Little Theatre

ATHENS
Ohio Valley Summer Theatre
Ohio University

BAY VILLAGE
Bay Village Players

BEREA
Berea Little Theatre
P.O. Box 265

BOWLING GREEN
Bowling Green State University
Theatre

Huron (Summer) Playhouse
c/o Mr. Elden Smith
Bowling Green State University

BRECKSVILLE
Brecksville Little Theatre

BRYAN
Bryan Playshop
c/o Eugene R. Comings
209 North Lynn Street

BUCYRUS
Bucyrus Little Theatre
P.O. Box 293

CANFIELD
Canfield Players
Community Building

CANTON
Players Guild of Canton
1717 North Market Avenue

CHAGRIN FALLS
Chagrin Valley Little Theatre

CINCINNATI
Cincinnati Music-Drama Guild

Cincinnati Valley Players
8304 Mayfair Drive

Northern Hills Little Theatre
2705 Oakleaf Avenue

Stage, Incorp.
Cincinnati Art Museum

CLEVELAND
Cleveland Play House
240 East 86 Street

Euclid Little Theatre
P.O. Box 4005

Karamu Theatre

COLUMBUS
Players Club of Columbus
547 Franklin Avenue

Village Little Theatre
First Community Church

COSHOCTON
Coshocton Footlight Players

DAYTON
Community Playhouse
Municipal Building

Dayton Theatre Guild
607 Belmont Park North

Experimental Theatre
141 West 3rd Street

Purple Masque
Shiloh Congregational Church

"Y" Players Theatre Group

EAST LIVERPOOL
Tri-State Theatre Guild

ELYRIA
Elyria Playmakers
P.O. Box 104

GREENVILLE
Greenville Art Guild Players

HURON
Huron Little Theatre
P.O. Box 154

LAKEWOOD
Lakewood Little Theatre
17823 Detroit Avenue

LEBANON
Lebanon Drama Guild
c/o Mrs. D. C. Maple
229 S. Mechanic Street

LIMA
Amil Tellers of Dramatics, Inc.

LORAIN
Lorain Community Theatre
1332 West 9 Street

MANSFIELD
Community Players
282 West 4th

Mansfield Little Theatre, Inc.
P.O. Box 51

MARION
Marion Little Theatre
c/o U.M.C.A.

MEDINA
Medina Masquers
Box 365

MIAMISBURG
Miami Valley Theatre Guild,
    Inc.
P.O. Box 11

NEW PHILADELPHIA
New Philadelphia Little Theatre

NORWALK
Milan, Norwalk Little Theatre,
    Inc.
c/o Vince Hipp
5 Benedict Avenue

OHIO (cont.)

The Shoestring Players, Inc.

OBERLIN
Oberlin Community Players
c/o Mrs. Eloise W. Fowler
53 North Park Street

PAINESVILLE
Studio Theatre

PENINSULA
Peninsula Players

PIQUA
Piqua Players Club
City Recreation Department

PORTSMOUTH
Portsmouth Little Theatre

SIDNEY
Sidney Theatre Guild

SPRINGFIELD
Civic Theatre & Country Playhouse
Box 57
The Play Box

TIFFIN
Hedges-Boyer Barn Theatre

TOLEDO
Toledo Center Players
2275 Collingwood

Toledo Dance Theatre
c/o Wm. Cottle
936 Post Street

Toledo First Nighters Workshop
2561 Charlestown

Toledo Repertoire Little Theatre
16 Tenth Street

Toledo Unitarian Theatre
3420 Middlesex Drive

URBANA
Urbana Community Players

WADSWORTH
Wadsworth Footlighters
312 Crestwood Avenue

WARREN
Trumbull New Theatre, Inc.
174 North Park Avenue

YOUNGSTOWN
Youngstown Playhouse
1497 Market Street

OKLAHOMA

BARTLESVILLE
Bartlesville Little Theatre Guild
P.O. Box 1573

OKLAHOMA CITY
Mummers Theatre
1108 West Main Street

TULSA
Tulsa Little Theatre
1115 South Delaware

OREGON

COOS BAY
The Little Theatre on the Bay
P.O. Box 722

EUGENE
Very Little Theatre
2350 Hilyard Street

FLORENCE
Florence Civic Theatre

HOOD RIVER
Hood River Civic Theatre
Route 2, Box 122

NEWPORT
Yazuina Players

OREGON CITY
Oregon City Little Theatre

PORTLAND
Portland Civic Theatre
1530 S.W. Yamhill Street

ROSEBURG
Roseburg Community Players
c/o YMCA Roseburg Armory

PENNSYLVANIA

ALLENTOWN
Civic Little Theatre, Inc.

ALTOONA
Altoona Community Theatre,
Inc.

BRIDGEPORT
Edgewood Theatre Guild

BROWNSVILLE
Brownsville Civic Theatre

CAMP HILL
The Cumberland Players

CARLISLE
Carlisle Players, Inc.

CHELTENHAM
Palette Players
Cheltenham Township Art Center
ter

CLEARFIELD
Old Town Players of Clearfield

EASTON
Lafayette College Little Theatre

ERIE
Erie Playhouse

FREELAND
The Freeland Stagecrafters

HARRISBURG
Harrisburg Community Theatre

HATBORO
Village Players of Hatboro

JENKINTOWN
Beaver College Theatre Playshop

LANCASTER
The M. Harriet Walker Players

LANGHORNE
Langhorne Players, Inc.

LATROBE
Latrobe Little Theatre
210 Commercial Bank Building

Mission Players
Mission Inn

LINCOLN
Lincoln University Players

MEADVILLE
French Creek Valley Players

MECHANICSBURG
The Little Theatre of Mechanicsburg
burg

NEW KENSINGTON
New Kensington Little Theatre
Box 730

PENNSYLVANIA (cont.)

PALMERTON
Neighborhood Players

PHILADELPHIA
Actors Stock of Philadelphia
YWCA—2027 Chestnut Street

Alden Park Players, Inc.
Alden Park Manor

Neighborhood Players
428 Bainbridge Street

Plays and Players

Stagecrafters
Chestnut Hill

PITTSBURGH
The Catholic Theatre Guild of
    Pittsburgh
P.O. Box 2023

Irene Kaufmann Settlement
    Curtaineer
1835 Center Avenue

P.C.W. Little Theatre
Pennsylvania College for Women

Pittsburgh Playhouse
222 Craft Avenue

Wilkinsburg Little Theatre
Box 8826

"Y" Triangle Players
Downtown YMCA
Wood Street

READING
Reading Community Players

RIDLEY PARK
The Barnstormers

SCRANTON
Little Theatre Guild
440 Wyoming

SWARTHMORE
Players Club of Swarthmore

WARREN
Warren Players
Box 563

WAYNE
The Footlighters, Inc.

WILKES-BARRE
King's College Players

Wilkes-Barre Little Theatre

YORK
York Little Theatre
153 North Beaver Street

RHODE ISLAND

NEWPORT
Newport Players Guild
Community Center
Marlborough Street

PAWTUCKET
Pawtucket Community Players
P.O. Box 75

WESTERLY
Westerly Players, Inc.

SOUTH CAROLINA

CHARLESTON
Dock Street Theatre, Inc.

Footlighters Players

CLEMSON
Clemson Little Theatre

COLUMBIA
Town Theatre

FLORENCE
Florence Little Theatre Guild

GREENVILLE
Greenville Little Theatre

ORANGEBURG
Loure Players

SPARTANBURG
Little Theatre

SUMTER
Sumter Little Theatre

SOUTH DAKOTA

RAPID CITY
Rapid City Theatre Guild
Room 227 Buell Building

SIOUX FALLS
Community Theatre

WATERTOWN
Town Players, Inc.

TENNESSEE

BROWNSVILLE
Brownstone Little Theatre
Exchange Club

CHATTANOOGA
Chattanooga Little Theatre
8th Street & Park Avenue

JACKSON
Jackson Community Playhouse

JOHNSON
Johnson City Little Theatre
    Players, Inc.

LYNCHBURG
Lynchburg Theatre

MEMPHIS
Memphis Little Theatre

NASHVILLE
Circle Players, Inc.
400½ Broad Street

OAK RIDGE
Oak Ridge Community Play-
    house
P.O. Box 563

SPRINGFIELD
The Community Theatre

TEXAS

AMARILLO
Amarillo Little Theatre, Inc.

AUSTIN
Austin Civic Theatre
2828 Guadalupe

CORPUS CHRISTI
Little Theatre of Corpus Christi

DALLAS
Margo Jones Theatre

TEXAS (cont.)

DENISON
Denison Community Players

FORT WORTH
B'nai B'rith Little Theatre
B'nai B'rith L.F. Shanblum
　Lodge

Wing and Masque Players
Convair Recreations Association

GALVESTON
Galveston Little Theatre, Inc.

HOUSTON
Alley Theatre

Houston Civic Theatre, Inc.
University of Houston

Houston Little Theatre

MIDLAND
Midland Community Theatre,
　Inc.
301 West Missouri

ODESSA
Permian Playhouse
903 Bernice

SAN ANGELO
San Angelo Civic Theatre

SAN ANTONIO
San Antonio Little Theatre
506 Billita Street

SHERMAN
Sherman Community Players

TYLER
Tyler Civic Theatre

UTAH

PROVO
Provo Players Guild
820 North 6, E. Provo

VERMONT

BURLINGTON
Burlington Theatre Club
Box 393

CHELSEA
Chelsea Hometowners

PLAINFIELD
Plainfield Little Theatre

RUTLAND
Rutland Players, Inc.

SPRINGFIELD
Springfield Community Players

VIRGINIA

ALEXANDRIA
Little Theatre of Alexandria
Box 1016

ALTAVISTA
The Little Theatre of Altavista

ARLINGTON
Arlington Players
Glebe Road at South 8th Street

BEDFORD
Bedford Little Theatre
Box 272

FALLS CHURCH
Falls Church Community Theatre
190 East Broad

HAMPTON
Hampton Little Theatre

LYNCHBURG
The Little Theatre of Lynchburg

NEWPORT NEWS
Little Theatre of Newport News
P.O. Box 226

NORFOLK
Norfolk Little Theatre

Norfolk Players Guild
912 Washington Avenue

ORANGE
Piedmont Players

PULASKI
Pulaski's Little Theatre, Inc.
538 Dora Highway

RICHMOND
Catholic Theatre Guild
305 North Third Street

The Masquers
Department of Recreation &
Parks

Monroe Center Players
Monroe Community Center
Peter & Leigh Streets

Richmond Civic Ballet
1815 Grove Avenue

Richmond Civic Theatre
c/o WRWA Hotel Richmond
9th & Grace Streets

Richmond Opera Group, Inc.
Route 13, Ridge Road

Shakespeare Players
Department of Recreation &
Parks

Summer Theatre
4106 Cary Street Road

VIRGINIA BEACH
Little Theatre

WASHINGTON

ABERDEEN
Aberdeen Community Theatre
City Hall

BELLINGHAM
Bellingham Theatre Guild

BOTHELL
Bothell Intercommunity Theatre
P.O. Box 698

CAMAS
Camas Little Theatre
632 NE Everett

LAKEWOOD
Lakewood Players

MOUNT VERNON
Valley Players
1203 East Division Street

OLYMPIA
St. Martin's Players

PULLMAN
Pullman Community Theatre

SEATTLE
Tryout Theatre

WASHINGTON (cont.)

TACOMA
Tacoma Little Theatre

Tacoma Theatre Guild

WALLA WALLA
The Little Theatre
Garden City Heights

WENATCHEE
Wenatchee Theatre Group
520 Yakima Street

YAKIMA
Little Theatre Group of the Yak-
    ima Valley Arts Association

WEST VIRGINIA

CHARLESTON
Kanawha Players
5315 MacCorkle Avenue

HUNTINGTON
Community Players, Inc.
Abbott Theatre
420 West 14th Street

MORGANTOWN
Morgantown Little Theatre
Box 588

WHEELING
Little Theatre of Wheeling, Inc.
Box 103

WISCONSIN

APPLETON
Attic Theatre

BARABOO
Baraboo Theatre Guild

Green Ram Theatre

BELOIT
Beloit Civic Theatre

BROOKFIELD
Brookfield Players, Inc.
Nana Lister, 10605 Hawthorn
    Lane

BURLINGTON
Burlington Haylofters
Malt House Theatre

DELAFIELD
Delafield Drama Group
c/o Helene Fierke

ELM GROVE
Elm Grove Players
12450 Elmhurst Parkway

FENNIMORE
Fennimore Community Theatre

FISH CREEK
Peninsula Players

FOND DU LAC
Fond du Lac Community The-
    atre
YMCA

GREEN BAY
Green Bay Community Theatre
Box 282

HALES CORNERS
Franklin Players
10035 West St. Martin's Road

HARTFORD
School House Players

JANESVILLE
Janesville Little Theatre
Box 341

KENOSHA
Little Theatre, Inc.
5515 Sheridan Road

MADISON
Madison Theatre Guild
255 Blount Street

MANITOWOC
Masquers Inc.
Coach House
Lincoln Avenue

MARINETTE
Twin City Players
607 Marinette Avenue

MENOMINEE
Menominee Theatre Guild
Mrs. John Sneesby
Oakwood Heights

MILWAUKEE
Center Players
1400 North Prospect

Milwaukee Players
1111 North 11th Street

Perhift Players
1400 North Prospect

YMCA Playhouse
915 West Wisconsin Avenue

NASHOTAH
Canterbury Players
Box 6

OSHKOSH
Oshkosh Community Players
1112 Elmwood Avenue

PHILLIPS
Phillips Community Theatre
475 South Lake

RACINE
Racine Theatre Guild
601 High Street

RHINELANDER
Tower Ranch Theatre

SUPERIOR
Superior Community Players
1014 Harrison Street

TOMAH
Tomah Little Theatre Guild
723 Lake

WASHINGTON ISLAND
Washington Island Players
Conan Eaton

WAUKESHA
Moor Players
Moor Hotel

Waukesha Civic Theatre
Box 221

WAUWATOSA
Curtain Club
Clyman & Fifth Streets

Wauwatosa Players
Village Play House

WEST BEND
West Bend Community Theatre

WHITEFISH BAY
Whitefish Bay Players
7338 North Navijo

WILLIAMS BAY
Belfry Theatre

WYOMING

CASPER
Casper Community Theatre
Box 417

CHEYENNE
Cheyenne Little Theatre Players
2803 Carey Avenue

SHERIDAN
Community Players